I'm Not Playing

Thoughts from a Raw Brotha

I'm Not Playing

Thoughts from a Raw Brotha

Rom Wills

Wills Publishing

I'm Not Playing
Thoughts from a Raw Brotha

Copyright © 2017
By
Romuald P. Wills

ISBN-13 978-0692956281
ISBN-10 069295628X

To my sons.

Also by Rom Wills

Ask me how I know.

\- Rom Wills

Table of Contents

Introduction

For me, it always comes back to writing. I remember a conversation I had years ago when I worked in a more corporate environment. I had a co-worker who was very gifted at reading people. I remember he looked at me and said, "Rom, you shouldn't be here. You should be in a room somewhere working on a novel." He knew that I had already written three books and that my passion was writing. I would eventually leave that job to focus on my craft. If I do say so myself I have an impressive body of work.

Over the years I have had two blogs. The first had a few followers and eventually I let that one die out. The second is the blog was with my current website, romwills.com. The blog was active between October 2013 and February 2016. Every Sunday I would post what a dear friend called, "very long essays." I had another friend who wouldn't drink her morning coffee until I posted my blog. She admonished me one morning for posting later than I usually did. She needed her coffee. I had many readers from all over the world who posted insightful comments both public and private. It was a great period.

Eventually I got tired of posting every Sunday and I needed a break. I posted a brief statement in early February 2016 saying that I was taking a hiatus until March 2016. When I came back in March instead of posting a blog I decided to post a YouTube video. I still didn't feel like writing but I had promised I would be back and as they say the show must go on. I used YouTube because I was too cheap to upgrade my website to post videos directly. It turned out being cheap would actually bring me much notoriety.

When I posted on YouTube I wasn't thinking in terms of people actually watching the videos on YouTube. I seriously thought people would only watch the videos on my website. What happened was that random people started commenting on the videos on the YouTube site. With the comments came subscribers. As the subscribers increased the demand for more videos came. It got to the point I stopped posting videos on my website and focused on the YouTube side of things. Even when I did that I still didn't get back to doing blogs. I simply replaced them with my now famous Sunday Morning Podcasts.

Now I'm making a name for myself with my videos and podcasts. People from all over the world are watching and listening to me. This has increased the sales of the books I have currently in circulation. Life has been very good to me. Despite everything at my core I'm still a writer. I'm still happiest sitting at a computer writing about whatever is on my mind at that moment.

The book you are holding in your hand is a collection of my most popular blogs from April 2014 through September 2015. Starting with my most popular blog ever, "Blowing it with Mr. Right," I address issues such as good men withdrawing from relationships, men who get multiple women, sexual subcultures, and my views on that thing called love.

One final note about the title and subtitle of this book. I've used two titles for the blog. One title was "I'm Not Playing." The meaning was that I was giving it to people raw and unfiltered which led to me using a second title which was "Raw Brotha." I felt it was appropriate to use both terms for this book.

Sit back, drink your favorite beverage, smoke a joint, which may be legal depending on which you live in, and enjoy reading my thoughts.

Blowing It with Mr. Right

April 12, 2014

"Where are the good men?" This is a universal question asked by millions of women. Whether in the news media, social media, living rooms, beauty salons, or bars, women want to find the good men. Men usually answer by saying, "I'm right here." Of course many women don't agree with the men. When you think about it there is a whole industry devoted to the concept that women have trouble finding "good men." There is another angle to this that is rarely discussed publicly. The angle is that many women will have a "good man" and leave the relationship.

Now understand where I'm coming from when I say women will leave a good man.   I'm not talking about a woman leaving some boring nice guy or an abusive asshole both of whom consider themselves good men.   I'm talking about women leaving men they consider to be Mr. Right. The women will have a great relationship and think highly of their men.   The women will be happy.   There will be minor problems that come up because both parties are human but nothing that can't be worked out.   Thing is though the couple can be happy, there are outside forces that can destroy a good relationship.   Let me give y'all a scenario based on real-life conversations I've had with hundreds of women and scores of men.

Freddie and Linda Doright have been married for five years with a young daughter.   Everything is good in their marriage for the most part.   They don't have the same excitement they had while dating but they still have a good time together.   There are some things that could be improved.   Freddie could be a little more romantic in Linda's eyes.   Instead of communicating this with him she talks with her girlfriends, Betty, April, and Doreen.   Her girlfriends are all single and have a tendency to bash men.

So they start getting in Linda's ear.   They magnify everything Freddie isn't doing right.   After a few months, they collectively tell Linda, "girl you deserve better."   Now Freddie is a hard worker, handsome, nice body, and committed to being a one-woman man.   The sex life is even good.   Yeah they could go out more but Linda never expresses her desire to do so.   Freddie thinks everything is cool.

*After listening to her girlfriends, Linda starts holding back on sex and minor things become major arguments.   After one major argument she tells Freddie he needs to leave.   So Freddie moves out and now they are separated.   Her girlfriends come over to console her.   After a few weeks they come over to take her on a "girl's night out."   So they're at the club having a good time and that's when **HE** walks up and introduces himself. Dexter. Dexter Goodbar.   Six foot, drop dead handsome, muscular, a stylish dresser, with a sexy walk.   Linda and her girlfriends had been checking out Dexter as he erotically danced with a woman on the dance floor.   Dexter sees that he has been chosen and thus makes his move.*

Dexter starts spitting that smooth game with that sexy voice. Getting Linda wet as he hits her with a verbal aphrodisiac and a piercing gaze.   Next thing you know Linda is going home with Dexter. They get to his place and Linda says, "You know I usually don't do this."   Dexter looks at Linda, grabs her hand, pulls her to him and kisses her fiercely.   Next thing you know the clothes are off and Dexter is doing her.   Not just doing her but doing her…WELL.   Linda has several orgasms.

After a month of sex with Dexter, Linda decides to file for divorce.   She's convinced she's found her soulmate.   She files the papers and tells Dexter.

Linda: I've filed for divorce from my husband.   We can be together now.

Dexter: Together?   Who told you it was like that?

Linda: We have something special together.   I want to be with you.

16

Dexter: You better get out of here with that shit.   I just wanted some pussy.   Don't get me wrong, you suck a mean ass dick but my other women got skills too.

Linda: I thought I was the only one?

Dexter: I ain't never tell you that.   You need to get your shit and go.

Linda: Just like that?

Dexter: Yeah just like that.

Linda leaves Dexter's place feeling depressed and humiliated. She is consoled by her girlfriends, April and Doreen.   She thinks she made a mistake in filing for a divorce.   She thinks she should try to reconcile with Freddie.   While talking with April and Doreen, Linda asks about Betty.   They say that Betty has pulled away them lately. They are not sure what's going on with her.   So where's Betty? Hmmmm.

While Dexter had Linda's ankles up by her head, Freddie was at his small place trying to make sense of everything.   All he was doing was going to work and coming home sleeping.   One day he is on a social media site and he gets a private message from Betty.   She asks how he is doing.   He said he's making it.   Betty said it's too bad what's happened and that Freddie is a good man.   Ironically Betty was the main one telling Linda she needed to leave Freddie.   They message each other a few more times and then talk on the phone.   Betty calls him one day and asks if she can come over for a few minutes because his apartment is on the way to an appointment she has.   Freddie without thinking says, "Yeah sure."

A few hours later Freddie hears a knock on his door, when he answers it he sees a stunning sight.   Betty is standing at his door with a short black dress on that shows off her perky breasts, hugs her round ass, and showcases her shapely legs. She has her hair done and some four inch heels. On top of that she is holding a plate of food talking about Freddie would appreciate a home cooked meal. Freddie takes the plate to the kitchen and when he gets back to the living room Betty has made herself at home on the couch. Freddie sits on the couch with her. Betty crosses her legs in Freddie's direction revealing just enough thigh to make a normally reasonable man stupid. Game over.

Actually it was game over when she was standing at the door with the plate of food.

A few weeks later Linda stops by to surprise Freddie and to talk about reconciling. Linda gets the surprise though when Betty answers the door in a silk bathrobe. In one moment Linda realizes she lost a good man.

This scenario is based on conversations I've had with the Freddies and Lindas of the world. I've had a **WHOLE** lot of conversations with the Bettys of the world. Scandalous women like and trust me for some reason. It's probably why I have a great understanding of women. But I digress. That's another blog.

See many women will have a good man and not even know they have a good man. Many women out here may excel at their careers and have a lot of book smarts but will lack street smarts. Many women grow up sheltered and may not have any significant contact with men until they are young adults and out in the world. They didn't run the streets. They weren't going to parties. Many went through high school without a boyfriend. They were usually the awkward girls, the ugly ducklings, the late bloomers, the nerdy girls. They weren't the party girls who have been sexually active since the age of ten and who ironically enough know a good man because they have a lot of experience with the bad ones. The party girls have game.

Many women will get married or in a relationship without having a lot of contact with men. I don't just mean sexual contact but contact period. Many women don't even have male friends or even male cousins around to truly learn about the male species. So they really don't have enough experience to know they got something good on their hands. An old school player told me when I was a teenager that he would rather marry a woman who has been with thirty men than one who has been with only two. His reasoning was that the woman who has been only two men would at some point get the urge to cheat because she would always wonder what she is missing out on. Whereas the woman who had thirty men knows most men aren't for her and would truly appreciate a good man.

Only a true player understands that wisdom. I learned the game from street cats and hustlers. Men who could read a person better than a psychologist because their lives depended on it. Keep in mind many Pimps end up marrying their top prostitute.

In the scenario Linda's marriage was wrecked by her "friends." Many women think the women they have around them have their best interest at heart. Women are very competitive with each other and very bitchy. Many women

19

will sabotage their "friend's" relationship because they hate to see another woman happy. Jealousy is a beast. Women will say they don't have a lot of female friends for this reason.

Another factor is that you have women who have no problem going after the husband or boyfriend of one of their friends. In fact, some women are so bad with this that you could introduce them to a single man who has everything going for him but they will reject him. Yet the man becomes desirable the second he's seen with a woman. Every single woman needs to take any advice about their man from another woman with a grain of salt.

Then there's that Dexter factor. Most women don't get a chance to get with that physically attractive man with the dripping sex appeal. There are women who had good men who provided for them and satisfied them sexually. The women would tell me they had good men and tell me how good they were. Then all of sudden that smooth man with the big chest and soothing voice walks into the scene and it's game over. There is a sub-population of men who have that type of sex appeal. Women meet these men and their common sense goes out the door. Some women have enough sense to limit their interaction with a Dexter to a fling. Many women, however, think there's something more there and leave a good man thinking there's a future with a Dexter. Of course they get their feelings hurt when they realize they were just a warm body to satisfy Dexter's lustful nature. A few women are lucky enough to get back with their men. Most lose out because the Bettys swoop in to get that man.

Straight up, many women need to stop complaining about a shortage of good men. Many women know they had a good man and they blew it by listening to their jealous girlfriends. They know they blew something good because they wanted to chase Mr. Goodbar.

The Good Man Rebellion

April 27, 2014

Back in the late 1990's I started working on a book
called "The Game." It was inspired by the classic book by
Ayn Rand, **Atlas Shrugged**. In **Atlas Shrugged**, a man
named John Galt said he would stop the engine of the world.
Galt convinced all the innovators and competent people of
the world to go on strike. Without these people the world
fell apart. They were the "engine" that kept the world
moving. Thus Galt stopped "the engine of the world."
Great concept. What if this was applied to male/female
relationships?

So I started writing "The Game" with this concept in
mind. What keeps relationships going? It is not the players

or bad boys. It is the good men who pick up the slack for the destruction caused by the players. It's the good men who step in to take care of the women and often her children after the bad boy has moved on to greener fields. It's the good men who work the steady jobs and volunteer to mentor and coach children. It's the good men who keep the community functioning. It's the good men women look for when they are looking for more stable relationships.

In "The Game" the main character "Enrique" said "he would stop the game." Enrique convinced the good men and even some players to withdraw from women romantically until things changed in relationships. Specifically until the games between men and women stopped. Enrique wanted to promote honest and authentic relationships. The book had a happy ending as the men and women came together and decided to work on healthy relationships. Too bad I couldn't publish the book.

A writer is powerful. The pen is mightier than the sword. A single idea can literally change the course of history. That's why repressive regimes try to control writers. In military coups, writers are usually among the first to be detained. I finished the first draft of "The Game" and was satisfied. The book would have been a bestseller. The book never saw the light of day. I didn't tell a soul what the book would be about other than the title. They thought it would be a book about how to play relationship games and I didn't bother to correct them. I looked at the book and realized that despite the solutions provided people would take things the wrong way. I saw that good men would read the book and actually go on strike. I couldn't responsibly start that type of movement.

Too bad it happened anyway.

Many men are refusing to interact with women in American society. These are not the loser, contributing nothing positive to society, parasitic type of men. The men who are withdrawing are the hardworking, responsible men who would step in to raise another man's child, who would love a woman despite her emotional baggage, or that she is plain looking or overweight. You have regular men who are refusing to interact with American women. The same American women who are complaining on social and mainstream media about the shortage of "good men." What the women should really say is that there is a shortage of Mr. Goodbars. This is something that is evident in ALL American social classes and racial groups.

Women have been discarded by enough Mr. Goodbars and then start to look for more stable men. Except the good men see through this now. The good men are communicating more through blogs and other social media so they know the game better. Men of all American racial groups have started active movements to separate themselves from specifically American women. They are refusing to pursue relationships with most women regardless of the women's level of attractiveness. These men are not stepping in raise another's man's children. They are not stepping in to be in a loving relationship with emotionally damaged woman.   They are withdrawing from women period.   Some of these men will go as far as to deride the men who DO want to interact with women as simps, manginas, and white knights.

The Good Man Rebellion is an issue that must be faced.   There isn't enough Goodbars or Successful Men to go around.   Quite frankly when the Goodbars and Successful Men decide to settle down for the most part it will only be with the women who rank in the top 5 percent of the female population in terms of physical attractiveness and femininity. Despite what most women like to think about themselves they are regular in the eyes of most men.   These regular women are the ones most being harmed by the Good Man Rebellion.

The Men Who Get the Most Women

May 4, 2014

Alpha males and bad boys. There is a multimillion dollar industry made up of seduction gurus and dating coaches who tell men, for hefty fees of course, how to get sex from women. In general men are taught how to be, well, alpha males and bad boys. These type of men are seen as the ones who get the most attention and sex from women. So it seems logical to emulate these men. The only real issue though is that alpha males and bad boys really don't get the most women and in many cases not even the best women.

See, there are a lot of misconceptions being promoted on the Internet regarding the act getting sex from women. Seduction gurus and dating coaches promote workshops, books, and videos telling men how to be players. The only problem is that the overwhelming number of these gurus and coaches have never been players themselves. These coaches are teaching men what men they thought were players were doing to get women. These coaches didn't live in a player's world but were from the outside looking in. The coaches in many cases didn't know what was really going on. Let me use basketball as an analogy.

I've been around basketball fans some of whom considered themselves knowledgeable about the game. I've also been around many division one (D1) college basketball players, a few of whom are now coaches at D1 schools. Now in conversations with fans they will talk about dunks, nice jumpers, and points per game. The D1 Players, however, would talk about playing defense, drop steps, cuts to the basket, balancing the floor, and blockouts. The fans could talk about the scoring and little else, and the D1 players would talk about the other things that made the game work. When I used to play pickup basketball games, the fans, who never had any organized basketball experience, would always pick me last, if at all. The D1 players would pick me right away because though I wasn't a big scorer they knew I was very good at other aspects of the game.

In the game of pulling women most seduction gurus are fans of the game and not actual players. Very few actual players are in the industry.

Now the big thing is teaching men how to be alpha males or bad boys. There's a lot of focus on teaching men how to simply meet women but this considered to be beginner stuff even by those in the industry. People are missing the mark on most cases as far as the men who get the most women.

Alpha males really don't get the most women. See a true alpha male is a leader, the top dog, the man. A man to being a leader means he is going somewhere in life. A man doing anything with his life does not have time to deal with a lot of women. Whether the alpha male is a corporate executive, a successful entrepreneur, or a street hustler he will be too focused on succeeding in his vocation to deal with many women. The true alpha male will have at most two women. In many cases he will have an inclination to be monogamous. Any man who deals with multiple women realizes that women can be a distraction if he is trying to accomplish anything. The true alpha male will have that one woman who will make a good mother and wife. She may or may not be physically beautiful but regardless her greatest contribution is supporting the man in his endeavors and keeping the family tight. He may then have a mistress who is content in her position. The job of the mistress is to provide pleasure to the alpha male.

True alpha males are not chasing a bunch of women around. They don't have time for that shit.

Another thing is that alpha males typically don't travel in circles where they can be casually observed. I did a book signing in the VIP section of a prominent nightclub in DC many years ago. The men had to pay a membership fee of several thousand dollars to have access to the VIP section. They were in there discussing business and chilling with women who were straight tens. I took a walk in the regular section of the club and felt an entirely different vibe. It was basically a bunch of average women and thirsty men. Now a few of the men were putting in work and to the untrained eye may have looked like alpha males but they weren't. Many dating coaches observe the behavior of thirsty men and think they are looking at alpha males. Then the dating coach will conduct a high priced seminar teaching men how to imitate thirsty men. See the problem?

Then there are the bad boys. Many men feel that bad boys get all the women. I can see why. The good woman with a bad boy is a popular theme especially in romance novels. Many men will see what they believe to be a good woman with a bad boy. Bad boys really don't get the most women or quite frankly the best women. In my nearly half century of living I have made one major observation about women who consistently get with bad boys. The women have serious mental health issues. I have NEVER met a woman who was reasonably sane get with a bad boy. Even on the low. When I say bad boys I don't mean someone who LOOKS like a bad boy with some tattoos and scruffy appearance. Many tattooed and scruffy men are among the best human beings you ever want to be around. I mean "actual threat to public safety" bad boys. Women who get with those men are in most cases marginally attractive anyway and from a personal standpoint aren't worth the trouble to think about. Many bad boy chasers lack class and it says something about the kind of men who find these women desirable.

Stop and think about that for a minute.

So it's not the alpha males who get the most women and not the bad boys. So who are the men who get the most women?

Much of the information in the media about the most desirable men is incorrect. Don't get me wrong, looks, money, and status will never hurt a man. At the very least if a man builds his body up and gets his economic program right he will get him a decent woman. I promote as much in my books. These things, however, will not attract a great number of women. Women reject men who have looks, money, and status all the time and not because they are nice guys. The women just didn't click with some men. There is no connection. The connection piece is the most important.

When I grew up I didn't learn how to pull women from the internet. It didn't exist at the time. I came of age of in 70's and 80's. I had to learn from trial and error and being in the presence of real players. I didn't have social media and videos. The men I learned from went against the prevailing "wisdom" we have today. Things really haven't changed.

First of all, these men would not be considered drop dead good looking. They had good body builds but almost never like a male model. Quite a few can stand to lose some weight or at least take an abs class. These men are never considered eye candy. They are decent looking at best. Many are described as "attractive in their own way" which is womanese for "he's not classically handsome but I'll ride him all night." They are not classic alpha males. Many are blue collar workers living modest lives. They are definitely not bad boys. They are very cool people and basically good citizens. So why do these men, who I call Lovermen, get the most women? Two reasons really.

The first is that these Lovermen are in touch with their male sexuality. Most men suppress their sexuality because of political correctness and religious indoctrination. The average man, especially nice guys, suppress their sexuality to the point where they don't make a woman's vagina tingle. Just like men are moved by a hard-on to approach a woman, a woman will respond to a man if he makes her vagina tingle. Despite what women say publicly, they are moved when they can turn on a man sexually. Even if it isn't a man they want. That's why many women will dress provocatively to get a men's attention. A few women can even have an orgasm based on nothing else but a man looking at her with lust. Many men don't realize this and try to act like they don't notice the woman's cleavage and big round butt. A mentor

31

once said that many men confuse the proper behavior for a man socially for the necessary behavior for a man sexually. The Lovermen make no attempt to suppress their sexuality. If they see a sexy woman, the sexy woman if she looks back will see the man's print. Ask me how I know.

The second reason is really the most important. It's one thing for a woman to find a man attractive be it physically or sexually. It's another thing for the woman to actually connect with the man. I alluded to the connection piece earlier. This is why alpha males and bad boys don't get the most women. Most true alpha males are picky. They tend to only want the best quality women. They go for the nines and tens. They may go for an eight if she brings other things to the table. Also many alpha males tend to be upper class or at least have aspirations to become part of the upper class. Most women are quite frankly average and content with a middle class existence. The average woman will have trouble connecting with a true alpha male regardless of her level of attractiveness because of class differences. As an aside most dating and relationship discussions do not take class differences into account. Bottom line the alpha male has a limited amount of women with whom he can form a connection.

With bad boys that class issue becomes even more apparent. Most bad boys come from poor and dysfunctional backgrounds. The women they tend to attract come from similar backgrounds. Cases of a woman coming from a middle or upper class background and hooking up with a bad boy are extremely rare. Even in situations where this seems to be the case, if one scratches below the surface they will see that a middle class woman may have grown up in a ratchet environment. Women tend to be most attracted to men similar to the boys they grew up around.

Lovermen tend to come from a background similar to the women they are dealing which is primarily middle class which quite frankly is a very big tent. There really isn't that much of a difference between the lower worker middle class and the more professional upper middle class. Both tend to work for other people and thus share a particular mindset. Lovermen tend to stay in their lanes. If a particular Loverman is rated as a seven by most women he will tend to only deal with women in the five to eight range. If a Loverman has an average face and twenty pounds of extra weight he will tend to deal only with average looking women with a little weight on them. Lovermen stay in their lanes and are cool with it. Too many men feel like they are entitled to women out of their leagues. The biggest scam out there are dating coaches telling men who rate as a five that after a few seminars they can get women who are tens. The Loverman has some common sense and doesn't waste his time chasing women out of his league. They are able to connect with women who are most similar to them. The best couples are always men and women who look similar to each other and have similar values.

With all the tools men have to meet and connect with women many are still having trouble doing something which

I personally consider to be easy. Women are not really that complicated. They try to act otherwise but I know better. A man don't have to be an alpha male to get the women. There are only a few alpha males anyway. A man doesn't have to be a bad boy. He needs only turn a woman on sexually and be able to make a mental connection to her. A man needs to become a Loverman.

Trumping Looks, Money, Status, and Game

July 13, 2014

So you have three men at a house party. Eric Money, Larry Gamer, and Dexter Goodbar. Eric is tall, handsome, and is dressed with a nice shirt and slacks. Eric speaks well and during his conversation with various women he makes sure they know what he does for a living, the car he drives, and that he lives in an expensive neighborhood. He has looks, money, and status. A couple of women are feeling him but most are ignoring him. Larry Gamer is doing his thing at the party as well. He's dressed casually and is average looking. Larry relies on his game as he talks to as many women as will stay still long enough to listen to him. Even though Larry projects an air of smooth confidence the women see through his façade and mostly ignore him. The only woman receptive to him is ugly, out of shape, and has the disposition of a water buffalo. Then there's Dexter.

Dexter is in the corner trying to eat some buffalo wings but different women keep coming up to him starting conversations. Dexter is handsome and built but isn't looking his best for the party. He needs a haircut and shave, wore average clothes, and says very little during the conversations. He doesn't tell the women he's a business owner or where he lives. When one woman asks about his occupation he tells her he's a store clerk. Dexter gets a little irritated because when one woman stops talking to him another takes her place. He really wants to finish his buffalo wings.

After the party Eric Money walks away with two phone numbers one of which shows real promise. Larry drives the water buffalo back to his mom's place. The next morning he will post on a player website about how he pulled a hot woman. Dexter put his number into the cellphones of ten women one of which gave him a blow job in an upstairs bedroom.

According to the dating coaches and seduction gurus Dexter should have been the one to lose out. There are two general schools of thought when it comes to men getting women. One school of thought is that men need looks, money, and status to get women. With looks, money, and status, a man is the Alpha Male, the dominant man all women are supposed to want. Another school of thought is that as long as a man has game he can overcome the lack of looks, money, and status.   There are strong arguments for both schools. Let's be real, they both work.   If a man has good looks, makes some money, and achieves a respected status he will get a fair amount of attention from attractive women. At the highest level of game a man will be able to manipulate attractive women into sleeping with him.   So how is Dexter trumping men who represents the two schools of thought?

At the party Dexter wasn't groomed or dressed his best.   He avoided telling women that he was a business owner.   He consciously negated the looks, money, status, method of attracting women.   He didn't use any game because he didn't approach any women and said very little to the women who approached him.   The woman who gave him a blow job was the sexual aggressor.   So what's Dexter's secret? Very simple. Dexter reeks of sexual charisma.   His very presence arouses most of the women who see him. Many of them are turned on to the point where they muster up the nerve to approach him.

A big issue in male/female relationships is that women only find a small percentage of men to be sexually appealing.   Most men feel that as long as they have money or game they can get women.   They will get a few women but in those cases the relationships tend to be less than harmonious. Other men feel as long as their looks are on point they will draw women.   They do but a common occurrence is that many women will lose interest in a good looking man once they get to know him.   Also many good looking men end up

37

with average looking women with bad attitudes. A man dripping with sexual charisma will have very beautiful women who will literally fight to get with him. Ask me how I know.

See sexual charisma is not a tangible thing. It's not about looks, money, or status. It's not about game and how many lines a man can use. Sexual charisma is an inner thing. It's a right brain thing. It's a spiritual thing. It comes deep from within a person. It's not something that is simply seen. It is felt by a person. Indeed a person who rates as a six on physical bone structure alone jumps up to a nine with sexual charisma. Women know what I'm talking about. From listening to conversations, reading articles, and lurking on message boards the average man is clueless about sexual charisma. Most men just see a woman's physical features and want to have sex with her. Somebody in tune like myself can make a distinction between a simply good looking woman and a woman with sexual charisma. Let me give an example.

I remember picking up my youngest son from school one day. I'm standing there chilling when a young woman walked past wearing sweats and a hat pulled down on her head. She wasn't dressed to impress. Now my preference is women in the 5'6" to 5'9" range with 40" hips. That gets me hot. This young lady was slim and only 5'4". Yet she literally dripped sexiness in her walk and demeanor. She had a stripper vibe to her even though she was though she was dressed like a bum. Another young lady I worked with had that same energy even though she was a sincere church girl.

Their sex appeal came out in their movements and demeanors. It wasn't something they tried. You could tell it was as natural to them as breathing.

A small percentage of men have that energy, that sexual charisma. Applying this knowledge to the four categories I talk about in my books, Nice Guys and Players, and Sexual Chemistry, it's easy to see the foundation of each type of man. The men in the Mr. Goodbar category have sexual charisma. I've said before that Mr. Goodbars tend to be good looking but not necessarily on the level of male models. Indeed many Mr. Goodbars would be killed in a "Smash, Marry, or Kill" thread on a social media site. In person, however, Mr. Goodbar wins because a woman would feel his sexual charisma. She would be moved not just by looks which is average for many Mr. Goodbars, but by the sound of his voice, how he looks at her, his body scent, and how he moves. Personally I've had women tell me that I had a sexy walk and that I dance erotically.

For a man to be considered Mr. Goodbar, the women around him need to consider him **SEXY**. That's it. Not fine, handsome, or even hot but **SEXY**.

The other three categories of men lack the sexual charisma of Mr. Goodbar. The Masked Man has the **SURFACE** qualities of what the media promotes as sexually appealing. To qualify as a Masked Man the man **MUST** be good looking. An average looking man with money is put into the Nice Guy category by women as I will explain later in this blog. In addition to being good looking the man must have money and status. Most male celebrities are Masked Men. Most male models are Masked Men. Many women are receptive to a very good looking man but will get turned off if he is stupid or bad in bed. Women are attracted to the mask because of the promise of sexual satisfaction. Women are disappointed once they see past the mask. I knew a man I'll call Peter. Peter was tall, handsome, and muscular. He was a professional who made six figures. Women would try to get his attention but lose interest after getting to know him. He even had girlfriends who cheated on him with Mr. Goodbars. I talked to one of the girlfriends. She confided that he was a dud in bed. Peter lacked sexual charisma.

The Nice Guy doesn't turn on the women at all. He feels like a brother to women. Many average looking men with money are put into the Nice Guy category. Money and status isn't what it was say fifty years ago. Since women can make their own money they don't have the same economic incentive to marry a particular man. It used to be that a woman would marry the man who showed the greatest willingness to provide for her. Women in general don't need that anymore. Women can afford to be pickier and to go after that broke man who can turn them out in bed. The pressure to marry isn't the same as it was back in the day. Many women will complain about the shortage of "good men." Despite this there are millions of men with money, education, and status who are having trouble getting a woman to say hi to them. The Nice Guy lacks the sexual charisma and above average looks.

The Gamesmen lacks the sexual charisma or above average looks to attract women to him. The general philosophy of the Gamesman is to approach as many women as possible. Indeed for the average Gamesman the concept of being routinely approached by women is alien. The Gamesman will come off to women as phony and persistent. They usually win, inconsistently, with basic and ugly women. If they get with beautiful woman it is usually low self-esteem on the woman's part rather than any game on the man's part. A few Gamesmen will amass a high partner count. These Gamesmen simply got real good at manipulation and figuring out which women are receptive to their game.

The four categories of men are simply how women see a man **SEXUALLY.** Most men, and ironically some women make the mistake of thinking that women don't want sex as much as men. No the social culture we live actively tries to control women's sexual expression. The average woman is sexually repressed. Women **WANT** to experience sexual pleasure but the social matrix shames them for doing so. Many men want a freak in the bedroom but because of their socio-religious indoctrination will shame a woman for actually being a freak in the bedroom. A woman isn't free to be herself sexually. That's when Mr. Goodbar comes in the picture. A woman is turned on by Mr. Goodbar because his **SEXUAL PRESENCE** not only sexually arouses the woman but communicates subconsciously that she can be free to be her **SEXUAL SELF.**

41

MR. GOODBAR FREES WOMEN SEXUALLY!!!

That sexual presence has nothing to do with looks, money, or status. Indeed looks, money and status enhances sexual presence. It has nothing to do with game. A man can pull a woman to him without saying a word. Let me share two examples. Back in the late 1990's I was a regular at this high end night club in DC. The club catered to an international crowd. There was this cat I'll call Vargas. He was tall, slim but muscular. He generally wore a muscle shirt and slacks. Not overly handsome because he had a pock-marked face. He wasn't outgoing and would stand in one spot the entire night. Women would go crazy over him. He had several women including Ethiopian women who would vie for his attention. This is significant because Ethiopian women in the DC area generally only dealt with Ethiopian men. Now a couple of Masked Men tried to copy his style and even though they were tall, handsome, and muscular, they didn't get the same attention from the women. In that same club it was routine for women to grab me and pull me to the dance floor. Not to brag but I got used to women approaching me in clubs back in the day.

Another example came when a few years ago I was at a hair expo selling copies of my books. This one Goodbar I'll call David bought a copy of my books. (For some reason Goodbars and Masked Men will buy my books and Nice Guys and Gamesmen will try to clown me.) Anyway he walked away from my table a woman called out to him and said, "Hey I want to take you home." David walked to her and said, "Put your number into my phone." She typed her number in and he looked at it and said, "This it?" She said yes and David walked away. I asked her about it after he left and she told me and her girlfriends who were standing there with her what she was going to do with him in graphic detail. David was more bulky than ripped, and he had locs and casual clothes on. There may be a looks argument but his money and status were not evident and he said very little to her so there was no game.

All my blogs, my books, and my coaching focus on increasing a man's sex appeal. Period. That's it. Many men have read my books and didn't like them because I don't give specific techniques for getting women. I say very little about cold approaching women. If a man develops his sexual presence women will find a way to approach him. If as a man you don't have above average looks, you don't make a lot of money, you lack status and you don't have the mindset for game you can still get attention from women. Indeed, a man who develops his sexual presence will find that money and status will come. Even someone into game will find it to be more effective if he is considered sexy.

When it comes to this matter I'm your huckleberry.

Goodbar Clans

July 20, 2014

So the star of the show in my books, blogs, and coaching is Mr. Goodbar. Well I write what I know. It's who I am. Actually women in the past have called me cocky, arrogant, player, bad boy, jerk, and those were the nicer comments. They called me sexy too so for some odd reason the other names didn't prove to be a hindrance to getting sex. That might have to be the "Being Mr. Goodbar" book I need to get around to publishing. Anyway Mr. Goodbar is in my blood as the men in my family had zero problems getting women. My great-grandfather was a minister that had the women in his congregation swooning. My paternal grandfather was a "whoremonger" as my grandmother called him. He knew a woman's body better than a doctor. My maternal grandfather was a smooth numbers runner who was a straight Mack. My maternal uncle as a cop looked like Billy Dee Williams with a personality like Alonzo Harris from Training Day. My father is a blue collar man who has women young enough to be my daughter chasing HIM. I have a couple of cousins who got paid by women for sex.

My point though is not to provide my family background. My real point is Mr. Goodbar isn't one single character type. The men in my family represent different types of Goodbars. My great grandfather was Black upper class while his daughter, my grandmother, married into a numbers running family. She in turn had a son who became a cop. My father's people were blue collar. My cousins were on that line between working class and Black Elite. All these men came from different places but represented different types of masculine sex appeal. In the manner of role playing games and young adult novels I have identified eight types of Goodbars or as I'll call them Goodbar Clans. What follows is a description of each group and their appeal to women. One thing I will point out is that in earlier blogs I talked about Lovermen, Demon Lovers, and Male Freaks. These titles don't constitute separate groups because they are traits that can be found in men in any of the clans.

One thing to note is that these clans are categorized according to how women are sexually turned on by them. For example a woman will be turned on by men in two of the clans but unmoved by men in the other five clans. There is no hierarchy in how these clans are presented. Think of them as different styles of sexual seduction.

LOOKERS

The Lookers are the pretty boys of the Goodbar Clans. These men are extremely handsome. They have been blessed with great facial bone structure, and in many cases pretty eyes. Lookers tend to have average bodies and be of average height. Women really don't care about a Looker's body. A few rare Lookers may be a few pounds overweight. Women are too busy staring at the face of a Looker to care about the rest of him. Lookers tend to take care of their face and will always have a fly haircut.

BODYMEN

Many women don't want to be around a man who looks better than they do. These women get turned on by a man with an average face and muscular body. The Bodymen are those cats with the killer physiques. They will have the big chest, broad shoulders, tall, muscular legs, and tight butts. Women say "dat ass" too. Women will want kiss the Lookers but will want to lick the chest and back of the Bodymen. Ask me how I know.

SWAG CATS

This clan is made up of men who are stylish dressers. These men will have fly glasses or shades. Maybe a nice gold chain. Cotton shirts or polos. Their pants will be pressed and creased. Rest assured their shoes will be shined to the point where you can see your reflection. Even when dressed casually these men will have on crisp jeans or athletic suits. Many women are turned on by a man who knows how to dress.

BAD BOYS

The Bad Boys are the Clan that catches the most hell. Many non-Goodbars think this group gets the most attention. Not really but they get enough. The Bad Boys tend to be decent looking with decent bodies. A big part of their appeal is their non-conformity. From a physical point of view they don't look like the mainstream population. Their hair will be longer. They will have more tattoos than the average person. They tend to make money in sometimes illegal ways or if legal outside the normal nine to five. Many may be artists.

COOL DUDES

The Cool Dudes are the charismatic Clan. They don't have the looks and the body. They are average dressers and they tend to be more mainstream. They are the men who can click with damn near everybody. Women are rarely turned on by the Cool Dudes at first. A woman may meet a Cool Dude and immediately put him in the friend zone. Then she talks to him for an hour and is ready to take him to a motel. The Cool Dudes know how to connect to a woman emotionally.

BANGERS

The Bangers are not necessarily handsome or have the best looking bodies. They tend to be built solid but not with muscular definition. Many may have a bit of a gut. They are not stylish dressers and are surprisingly conformist. They are very down to earth. The thing about them is that they look like they would fuck the shit out of a woman. The Bangers tend to be the men women go to when they just need to some good dick. Many people think women go to the Bad Boys or Bodymen for straight sex. Naw they go to the Bangers. See the other groups tend to be picky and will limit their sex partners to women who rate as an eight or above. The Bangers will fuck anything female. And they will do it WELL. These men aren't making love with candles and rose petals. Some women just want straight pounding and the Bangers happily oblige them.

THOROUGHS

The Thoroughs don't necessarily turn on women from raw sex appeal in terms of face and body. The Thoroughs turn on women because of how they handle themselves in life. The Thoroughs turn on women because they are confident and aggressive in how they approach life. These men are natural leaders. Most women and men for the matter were built to follow. The Thorough is the man who will always take the lead. He will take charge of a situation without thinking about it. Women will

unconsciously submit to a Thorough.   Many women are
turned on sexually if they submit to a man.

TANTRA BROTHAS

The eighth clan is a recent creation starting in 2007.
There is a tiny but slowly growing subculture of primarily
Black men who are learning how to bring a woman to orgasm
without touching them.   They are doing this through energy
projection. For the most part these men look like Nice Guys.
These men don't have game.   As a result of learning energy
techniques as well as going through some other regimens
women are being sexually aroused by these men by simply
being in the same room.   I estimate the number of men
doing this to be less than 100 right now.   In another ten
years the numbers may be in the thousands.

****

So there you have it. If you look at the clans any man
can become a Mr. Goodbar.   Many men will say that they're
ugly, or short, or broke and thus will not attract women.
Other than the Lookers, the Goodbars aren't the most
handsome.   Only the Bodymen have killer physiques.   The
other clans are made up of average looking men.   The only
thing they all have in common is sex appeal.   A man can be
ugly, short, and broke and still get sex as long as he is a Cool
Dude or Thorough.   He can still dress well like a Swag Cat.

The Tantra Brothas are mostly nerdy in behavior and physical appearance. Yet many of them have multiple women.

It's all about self-improvement. Many of the men in the Mr. Goodbar category didn't start off that way. One Looker showed me pictures of him that were very nerdy. When I met him he was modeling. Every Bodyman had to pick up that first weight. Every Swag Cat had to take years to develop their personal style. Every Bad Boy had to make a decision to be a non-conformist. Every Cool Dude had to talk to that first girl. The Bangers had to have that first sexual experience. Every Thorough had to develop his confidence. The Tantra Brothas had to learn their techniques.

If a man wants to become a member of one of the clans he has to be willing to do the work.

The "It" Factor, Part 1

August 10, 2014

Something that has fascinated me since the mid-nineties has been people with natural sex appeal. Anyone who has read my books and blogs can probably see that. What I have observed all of my life and really started paying attention to in the mid-nineties was the reality that the people considered the most sexually appealing are very rarely considered the most handsome or beautiful. I remember a talk show back in the day had some men on talking about this one woman who they found irresistible. The way they were talking you would think that the woman was drop dead gorgeous. When the woman came out she was a Plain Jane. The men on the stage and a few in the audience were going crazy over her. She had that "It" factor.

In a previous blogs and books I talk about sexual charisma. I had this to say about the subject in my book, Sexual Chemistry:

Brenda is a young lady who is in pursuit of a mate. She is invited to a singles party and while there she is introduced to four different men. The four men represent each of the categories. The men on the surface seem very similar. The men aren't movie star handsome but they are all decent looking with good body builds. Each man has developed at the very least the physical component of sexual chemistry. Yet, Brenda zeroes in on Mr. Goodbar. Mr. Goodbar doesn't look better than any of the men nor is he better dressed. Mr. Goodbar wasn't showing as much interest in Brenda as the other men. So why did Brenda zero in on Mr. Goodbar? There is ONE single trait that separates Mr. Goodbar from other men. That trait is sexual charisma. Without this trait Mr. Goodbar would be just like every other man.

In the chapter on the components of sexual chemistry I talked about the importance of charisma. Charisma, particularly sexual charisma, is the **X-FACTOR** *needed for a man, and a woman as well, to truly attract the right mate. This charisma will enhance everything else a person has going for them. It will make a person seem handsomer or prettier, sexier, and funnier. Quite frankly people will work harder to stay with a mate who has sexual charisma than one who doesn't. Lack of sexual charisma is why Masked Men must wear* *masks, Gamesmen must play games and Nice Guys are passed over. Sexual charisma is why Mr. Goodbar gets away with what he does.*

Often we will observe a man or woman who can break all of the supposed rules and still attract mates like crazy. No matter what line they use, what they are wearing, or how much money they may not have, they will still attract attention to themselves. Sexual charisma is very powerful. It has a physical effect on people. People can actually feel sexual charisma. A person's hormones will begin to act on their own. A woman may feel butterflies in her stomach or according to some reports, twitching in her vagina. Men may become so relaxed that they get an erection. Sexual charisma is an aphrodisiac.

When women encounter a Mr. Goodbar their hormones will kick in to make them more relaxed and receptive to what Mr. Goodbar has to say. Mr. Goodbars make great salesmen for this reason. Women, for the most part are defensive around men they don't know. Mr. Goodbar makes them comfortable, which in itself is important for a woman's arousal. There are married men who cannot make their wives comfortable.

I believe sexual charisma can be developed as I wrote in an earlier chapter. The key is for the man to make a serious effort to develop this trait. Nothing is impossible for a man committed to self-improvement.

Sexual Chemistry Pages 91-92

****

53

The thing I've observed the most over the years is that the sexiest men and women are very rarely the most facially attractive. It's hard for me to judge the facial attractiveness of a man but in conversations with women chasing a particular Mr. Goodbar they will often say, "He's not the best looking," but they will be in love with him. Indeed most women will make a distinction between a handsome man and a sexy man. Think about it, when a woman says a man is handsome AND sexy she is making a reference to two different qualities. Many men will wonder why women don't seem to want them even though they consider themselves handsome. The reality is that many good men are seen as handsome by women. Handsome doesn't equal sexy. Being called handsome is really generic. Now an extremely handsome man may be considered sexy but those types of men are rare.

Now from a man's point of view the women who get the most attention from men are very rarely the most facially attractive despite what men may say publicly. Men will definitely chase a beautiful woman but if one were to really pay attention, the women who get the most men are not the ones with the beautiful faces. An observation I've made is that many very beautiful women are lonely because for many reasons men don't approach them as much. Some of it simple intimidation but another part is that even many men are not consciously aware of is that many physically beautiful women are not sexy. They look good but they lack that "It" factor that will give a man a hard-on. Something that's not talked about a lot is that many men will marry a physically beautiful woman and then cheat with a sexy woman who may be physically homely.

So what gives a person that "It" factor? Part of it is physical. The face is the least important physical wise. Yes, there are people turned on by someone's face but it is rarely the most important consideration sexually. The body is the most important for turning someone on sexually. Think about it, buttafaces rarely lack for sexual companionship. See the body has an intelligence separate from someone's conscious intelligence. When a man and woman talk to each other they may consciously be talking about politics but on a subliminal level their bodies are having another conversation pertaining to sexual compatibility. If they are compatible he will likely get a hard-on with an increase in adrenaline, testosterone, and his breathing will change. Her vagina will tingle and her skin will become cold as blood rushes to her pelvic region. A man who is present with the women in his environment may notice the changes. Let me give a personal example.

Last week I had jury duty. Even though many people show up to jury duty dressed very casually I decided to look nice. So I'm in the jury lounge with a nice and crisp white dress shirt, creased slacks, and shined shoes. Now I'm chilling, reading a book. Being present I observed the reaction of the women around me. A young woman sitting next to me started twitching and crossing her legs in my direction. Eventually she turned her torso slightly in my direction. Maybe three women sitting across from me were having the same reaction as they looked at me and smiled. One even said hello as I looked up from my book. Now keep in mind I'm not saying a word to these women. My body however was having some interesting conversations with their bodies. So a key component to having the "It" factor is the body.

Now I have said publicly that I would not teach game unless I needed to get a point across. Let me give the reader some deep subliminal game dealing with the body. When a person is attracted to a particular body part they are not really attracted to that body part per se but rather to what that body part represents subconsciously. Every body part represents a personality trait. A person that is attracted to legs is really attracted to a person who is down to earth and connected with the real world. A person attracted to a person's pelvic region, (butt, penis, lower pelvis) is attracted to a person's creative nature as well as their natural sexual nature. A man attracted to breasts is attracted to a woman's nurturing nature. A woman attracted to a man's chest and arms are attracted to his protective nature. Many women are attracted to a man's shoulders. This means they are attracted to a man's ability to "shoulder" responsibility. A man attracted to a woman's neck is attracted to her refined nature. Being attracted someone's face or hair means that one is attracted to a person's spiritual nature. That why I say the face is the least important factor. I meant it in terms of carnal sex appeal. People who tend to be attracted to the face above everything else tend to be sexually repressed as far as the carnal/physical aspect of sex is concerned. I may address this in a future blog.

So for someone to have the "It" factor they need to have at least a decent body build. I'm going to be straight up. Fuck political correctness. Anyone who is serious about increasing their sex appeal needs to work on their weight issues. I'm not saying you need to be super-muscular or built like a swimsuit model but there is nothing sexy about being overweight. Within everyone's DNA blueprint there is an optimal body build which will naturally arouse members of the opposite sex. This blueprint is so intelligent that it will not only cause members of the opposite sex to be sexually attracted to you but will **ONLY** attract **COMPATIBLE** members of the opposite sex. The current obesity epidemic is not natural and is the enemy of not only sex appeal but of human evolution itself. People are not going to want to have sex with someone they find unappealing.

Now I know there are some men who are "chubby" chasers and women feel like being overweight is what these men want. The reality is that these men consider these women to be easy targets. If a video vixen woman made herself available to these men they would all of a sudden stop being chubby chasers. In cases where you see an in-shape man, say Mr. Goodbar, with an overweight women there are three things usually going on. One is that they got together when she was in shape and he loves her enough to stay loyal. Two, he's on some gigolo shit where she's giving him a place to stay or she's coming out of her pocket with some money for something. Three, he just don't give a fuck where he sticks his dick. Refer to my blog on Goodbar Clans and read the description for "Bangers."

Now this is one subject I will definitely do another blog on. I may even do a video because people are dancing around this subject out of fear of offending someone's sensibilities. When I look at the overall relationship problems in society, such as single mother homes, loneliness, sexual assault, and broken dysfunctional families we have to look at **ALL** the factors. Most women aren't single because they can't find a good man. I've challenged women on this issue for years. The average woman has about three handsome, responsible, decent, **SINGLE** men in their social circles. The problem is that the women do not consider these men to be **SEXUALLY APPEALING.** The good men are not built a certain way. They aren't built like Mr. Goodbar. To get an idea what women are chasing after, do a web search on "Male Exotic Dancers." Check any dancer videos. The women are going crazy over them. I've known several male dancers over the years. I was even offered a chance to become one. That's another story. If you look at them they don't look like male models facially but their bodies are on point. Several women have told me that they rejected particular men because they were overweight.

There's a big deal about men going to other countries for sex tourism. In the African-American community there has been a lot of chatter about successful Black men going to

58

places like Brazil and the Dominican Republic for sex tourism. That's part of it but many men are also looking for a certain type of woman. They are looking for **SEXUALLY APPEALING** women. The truth of the matter is that an American man regardless of race can find a woman with the personality qualities he wants right here in the country. The real problem is that many of the men are not physically attracted to the women most compatible to them. They are turned off by increasingly overweight women. Before a woman cries foul read the previous paragraph. Many women who would cry foul over what I just wrote are the main ones putting money in "Mandingo's" G-string and then meeting them back at a hotel. Ask me how I know. Don't mess with me on this, the real game is **DEEP** and I know it because I lived it.

Now the physical piece is simply the first part of having the "It" factor. My next blog I will talk about the mental aspect.

The "It" Factor, Part 2: Being Nice

August 17, 2014

So a person is physically attractive. They are handsome/beautiful with a sexually appealing body. People would say they have that "It" factor. Not necessarily. Many men have met women who were physically attractive with pretty faces and curves in all the right places. Then they talk with the women and are generally turned off. The woman is bitchy, stupid, or lame. Superior men will usually walk on by. Men of lesser quality may try to use the woman for their personal gratification. Many women meet physically attractive men who are tall, muscular, and have a nice print. Then they are turned off once the man starts talking. They will say, "He was all right until he opened his mouth." Another scenario is when they meet a good looking man who is arrogant. Some women may still deal with him but the arrogant man still doesn't have the "It" factor.

For a person to have that sexual "It" factor they must have a sexually appealing body. This is only half the equation. The other half of the equation are mental. It's really not that deep. The men and women who have that "It" factor have one thing in common: they are very cool people.

See there is a fucked up perception that bad boys and bad bitches get the most attention. They do get attention but usually for their physical appearance. What's not said though is that many bad boys and bad bitches get rejected a lot too. Contrary to popular belief the average bad boy does not have a harem. They usually have one or two women who are feeling them at any one time. The man with the "It" factor will have twenty women, including married ones, feeling him. As far as bad bitches they might have one serious dude who is using them for their bodies. Otherwise they tend to have several tricks and simps chasing after them for sex.

The men and women with the "It" factor tend to be very nice people. That's it. When I say nice I don't mean that sucker type of nice where a man or women is playing a role in order to impress the opposite sex. I'm going to say it bluntly, many Nice Guys are undercover assholes. Many Good Girls are undercover bitches. "Nice" for these people is simply a game tactic. The issue is that it rarely works for men and thus why there are so many bitter "nice" guys. They are like that dude who gets picked last or not at all for pickup basketball games. Even when they get in the game they suck. Many Good Girls put up a cooperative and even submissive front at first. Then when they get in there good with a man their true colors start to show. A man will think he has a virtuous woman until he accompanies her to her high school reunion and discovers that for some reason all the men are trying to get her alone and all the women seem to hate her. I roll my eyes when someone tell me how nice or good they are. If you are nice and good you don't have to tell anybody. Your actions will speak for themselves.

Stop and meditate on that. For real I never tell anybody I'm nice or good. I tell them my name, "Rom with an m" and keep it moving.

The man or woman with the "It" factor are genuinely nice people. They are authentic. They like people. They are able to get along with a wide variety of people going across racial, economic, religious, and subcultural backgrounds. People with this gift, yes it is a gift, exude a powerful charisma. Consider the following excerpt from my book **Sexual Chemistry:**

The second step in developing charisma is quite simply learning to treat all people the same way. This is probably the toughest thing for anyone short of spiritual leaders to do. Nevertheless there are people who accomplish this and as a result they exude charisma. What do I mean when I say treat all people the same way? Let me explain.

The vast majority of people walk through life with certain conditionings. As a result of these conditionings they will have certain judgments about people based on race, class, religion, haircuts, body shapes, etc. These conditionings will cause a person to like or dislike people who fit a particular criteria. For example, Tom is from an upper middle class African-American family. In his mind the only people worth anything are those from the same background. When he meets people from his background he is friendly, outgoing, generous, and overall he exudes a certain charisma in these situations. Now when Tom is with people from different backgrounds or races he is unfriendly, reserved, and overall will not exude any type of charisma. In these instances Tom is treating different groups of people differently according to his conditionings and his perceptions. This hurts Tom because to truly succeed in life he is going to have to deal with people who are from different backgrounds than his.

This dynamic can also be applied to how men deal with women. In a later chapter I will address more in depth the issue of how men should respond to women they consider attractive. With regard to the development of charisma, men will exude or at least try to exude more charisma with women they consider beautiful and sexy than with women they consider unattractive. As a result they will treat the beautiful woman more favorably than the less attractive woman. This is understandable but also a big mistake. Selective treatment like this only hurts a man in the long run as he may miss out on a very good woman.

Treating people differently according to one's own conditionings has a tangible effect on how others perceive us. For example, when John sees women he considers attractive he will speak with a deeper voice, walk more confidently, and will carry himself with a high and mighty attitude because he believes that this will attract the women to him. He is a Masked Man. When he is around less attractive women John is more genuine and honest.   In other words he is more down to earth.   What John doesn't realize is that when he acts high and mighty he actually turns women off and that they would probably prefer him if he was more down to earth.   In John's mind, however, he tells himself he has to walk and talk a certain way to get certain women when that is not the case. The key is to treat ALL women the same way. The best way to do this is not to think about it and just do this as a natural part of your personality.

The vast majority of people have an emotional condition to certain scenarios in life.   A woman, April, for example, may want a rich husband, so that when she is around men she thinks are rich she will walk and talk in a more seductive manner. Her emotional condition – wanting a rich man - causes her body and personality to react a certain way when she is around rich men. Now flipping the situation over, the same woman, April, with the emotional condition – wanting a rich man- will walk and talk in a less seductive and more defensive manner when around men she thinks are poor.

The mind is a powerful thing. When we have thoughts, likes, dislikes, about certain people and certain situations our bodies will react accordingly. Our body language says a lot. The way we walk says a lot. The way we dress says a lot. All of this creates an aura that is projected to the people around us.   It's been said that a picture is worth a thousand words. Think of a person's aura the same way.   The only difference is that a person's aura is constantly changing according to a person's emotions and circumstances of a particular moment. In some of these situations a person may have a charismatic aura, while in other situations the person's aura may be non-charismatic.   In order for a person's aura to be charismatic all the time they must not have a *condition attached to different circumstances. In other words, they must be able to approach every situation with an open mind. A man will have charisma if he exudes the same sexual energy around both beautiful women and less attractive women. The only way to do this is to not TRY to do this. What typically happens is that a man will see an attractive woman and will immediately start thinking of his approach, how his voice will sound, how he walks, what line he will use etc. His mind is telling his body to behave a certain way when it might not have been necessary. The truly charismatic man will see an attractive woman and let things flow. He will come off as more genuine and down to earth, which brings us to another factor in charisma.*

If one were to examine anyone who truly exudes charisma, especially sexual charisma, one will find that these people are very genuine and down to earth. In other words they're real.

Sexual Chemistry pages 58 – 61

****

There are men out there who feel like women like jerks. They see the jerk winning. The problem is that they are looking at the jerk's behavior. That's what they see. When I look at the same situation I look at the jerk's body build, his clothing, his car, and listen to him to gage his social class. Then I look at the woman and calculate the real reasons she is with him. When I was younger and grimier I would figure out how long it would take to run up her doggy style. Women who are bitchy usually have men who just want their bodies. I knew a bitchy, frumpy woman who I'll call Gretchen. She had a bad attitude, dressed poorly, and could be very unpleasant to be around. She was generally nice to me though. Any given time there was always two or three men trying to get at her. She didn't have the "It" factor but she was built like a brickhouse. Women like her might as well be sex dolls.

My point is that people look at the wrong thing so they feel being mean works. Naw. Try being a bad boy or bad bitch being ugly and overweight. It won't work.

Now by being genuinely nice and having the ability to get along with people allows a person to **CONNECT** with a potential mate. A person can have a handsome/beautiful face, a killer body, and stylish clothes. A man can make six or seven figures with a big house and late model car. A woman can be the best homemaker around. None of these things matter if someone cannot **CONNECT** on a personal level with another human being. There are plenty of people out there like that.

The reality is that very few people are going to consistently connect or even be around people who share their precise racial, social, religious, and economic backgrounds. If you go into a party with 100 people. Let's say that they are of the same racial group. Beyond that there are up to 100 different subcultures represented in the room. For example Greg goes to a party. All the women are Black. He talks to a few but has trouble connecting. Greg is from a working class background, he practices a Kemetic spiritual system, and he is self-educated. Most of the women are upper middle class, belong to different Protestant denominations, and have advanced degrees. The problem isn't so much the women as it is Greg who has biases against these types of women so he has trouble connecting. Brad, on the other hand has a similar background and beliefs as Greg but he is able to connect because he doesn't have pre-judgments about the woman based on their background. He finds that the women are very down to Earth and open to meeting and talking with men like him. These women are looking for genuine nice men.

I don't write any of these things based simply on my own personal experiences. I've known a few hundred men and women in my life who have had that "It" factor. They were the least judgmental, least biased, most open people I have ever met. They were the type of people who make a total stranger feel like they are their best friends.

It's not that difficult a concept. A person wanting to develop an "It" factor need to first make their bodies more sexually appealing and then work on being authentically good people.

Culture Clash - Sexual Subcultures

September 21, 2014

Let me share something about myself. One of my great interests is studying subcultures. Growing up I was exposed to different groups of people and their nuances. It fascinates me how people will deal with certain matters in different even contradictory ways due to their subcultural perceptions. In my last blog I wrote about subcultural differences in Black relationships. That was just the focus of the blog.　The same analysis can be applied to any racial or ethnic group.　There are also literally hundreds of what I would term to be "sexual subcultures."

When people see the term "sexual subculture" they will probably immediately think of the LGBT Community or the numerous Fetish communities.　Those are indeed the most public.　The subcultures I'm thinking about are not as well-known because people might not think of them as subcultures and many are not as organized.　Indeed some should be considered more like sub-populations.

The reason I'm even writing about this is because of my nearly eighteen years of being in the relationship self-help industry.　One observation I've made is that most books, seminars, and workshops approach relationships as if everyone is on the same page and has the same goals. That's why, despite all of the information out there from psychologists to old school player comedians, relationships seem to be getting worse.　One of my mentors said that the average length of male/female relationships has gone from three years to six months.　I have to agree with him.　I won't even get into the divorce rate.　In order to deal with these issues we need to break things down more.　We have to realize that there are indeed different sexual subcultures and subgroups and this will have an effect on the relationship landscape.　Let me get into some examples.

As I said there are literally hundreds of these sexual subcultures.　I remember back in the early nineties a friend of mine at my gym invited me to his place for a party.　Now he was Black so I naturally assumed I would walk into his basement apartment and see a bunch of fine ass sistas. Naw. I walked in and saw some very beautiful women. Every single one was Scandinavian primarily from Denmark. I had stumbled into a small social group that had Black men who would be otherwise be considered lame or corny to the average American Black woman looking like Macks with very attractive Danish women. It was an interesting experience because there were certain modes of behavior and protocols that were unsaid and yet still followed.

Speaking of sexual subcultures with interracial dynamics there is one sub-population known as "Queen of Spades." These are white women who desire sexual relations with Black men or BBC's (Big Black Cock). These women are identifiable by a Queen of Spades symbol from playing cards tattooed somewhere on them. There is a rough equivalent of Black women who desire white men, though as far as I know there isn't any symbols that identifies this subculture. Their detractors, particularly Black men, refer to them as "Negro Bed Wenches." Quite frankly many of the sexual subcultures deal with interracial sexuality.

Several of the sexual subcultures simply deal with what I would call body fetishes. You have the men who are called "chubby chasers" who are sexually attracted to overweight women. A subgroup within the chubby chasers are sexually turned on by feeding an overweight woman. Quiet as it is kept there are women who are turned on by Big Handsome Men (BHM). In the Black community Big

Handsome Men are called Teddy Bears. All women don't necessarily want that man with six pack abs. Some love a little bit of gut on a man. You have women who like very slim men.

One interesting thing I have found over the years is that these subcultures are not just about identifying symbols and shared cultural rituals and social customs. Often the thing that marks someone as a member of a group is their perceptions that they share with other people. It's not that they come together and say "we're a group." They just meet like-minded souls and because their perceptions are validated by others a subculture may indeed develop. Let me provide an example from my books.

In my books, **Nice Guys and Players**, and **Sexual Chemistry,** I divide the male population into four very general groups. I say very general because each group can be broken down until there are literally hundreds of subgroups. The four general groups are Mr. Goodbar, Masked Men, Gamesmen, and Nice Guys. Though initially someone may feel that these are arbitrary labels over the years I have observed that the labels are more than superficial. Each general group has a specific perception of life in general, and male/female relationships in particular. Let me share why I say this.

I've sold many copies of my books at trade shows, expos, book signings, and even in flea markets. I've picked up on something very fascinating. Each group reacted to my books differently. Indeed I got to the point I could look at a man, assess which group he was in, and predict whether or not he would buy the book. I even calculated how much salesmanship I would need to employ.

With the Goodbars I would barely need to open my mouth. I've lost count of how many times a pretty boy, bad boy, or Alpha Male would walk up to my table, look at the book, and break their wallet out and pay without saying two words. The ones who would talk would go through the books and say "that's me." My favorite was when this Hispanic dude I'll call "Rico Suave" bought the book. This cat approached my table with a crew. He was a pretty boy Alpha Male. Dude looked fly from head to toe like he stepped out of a modeling shoot with a silk shirt and creased slacks. A woman would have got wet from just his leather slip-ons. His haircut looked like it was nothing less than $100. He walked up, picked up my book, and said in smooth baritone, "Now THIS is who I am!" If someone saw this on a reality show they would say it was staged. That's how it went with Goodbars. Even to this day they are my biggest supporters.

The Masked Men would buy the books after some salesmanship on my part. Usually they would try to play it off like they didn't need the book and were just "supporting a brotha." The Gamesmen would tell me they didn't need the book because they already knew what was in the book. Some would even give me a look that said, "He don't know anything about game."

Ironically the men I wrote the book for, Nice Guys, would reject me outright. The few who would buy the book usually had the most criticisms if they saw me somewhere else. My favorite was one self-proclaimed Nice Guy who told me in so many words that my book was crap and everything I said was wrong. The irony is that my girlfriend at the time was at the table with me and this Nice Guy was checking her out while trashing my book.

The look on his face when I introduced her as my girlfriend was priceless. He slinked away after that.

Anyway the issue wasn't so much whether I was right or wrong. It was the perceptions of the men buying the books. See each category of man developed a certain perception of based on their interactions with women growing up. As they got older and in the world they naturally gravitated to people with similar perceptions. These men naturally created subcultures based on their perceptions.

Mr. Goodbar types typically started off as cute boys or star athletes. They were the popular ones in middle and high school. Even the bad boys tended to be either cute boys or athletic. These boys had little girls scheming on them almost from childhood. Let me share a funny thing that happened yesterday. I went to a flea market with my two sons to get some Shea Butter. As we were walking a cute little multiracial girl said hi to my youngest son and he totally ignored her. She got a "How dare he ignore me look" on her face. I chuckled. Prime example of how Goodbar rolls.

Goodbar discovers during his teen years or for late bloomers early twenties that despite what women say otherwise, women get open off a man's looks or body.

My point is that Mr. Goodbars are typically laid back when it comes to women because their perception is that women will always approach and hand them the pussy. Goodbars get in trouble with women who are not moved by their looks because the average Goodbar never had to develop any seduction skills. Goodbars will tend to hang with other Goodbars because of shared perceptions. Currently there is no real organized subculture of Goodbars because quite frankly there are very few of them relative to the rest of the population. As one Goodbar pointed out to me, "Except for college towns with big football programs how often do you see muscular men walking around?" A personal trainer on YouTube stated that only 1 in 20,000 men have six packs abs.

With Masked Men they weren't the cute and popular boys. Some may have been athletes though but not necessarily the star or the most handsome. The Masked Men were the smart boys who still had some level of cool in their middle and high schools. They grew up with the perception that they had to have something extra to attract women. Often they don't develop that extra until their thirties. The Masked Men may have had girlfriends in high school but probably not to the extent as Goodbar. The Masked Men realize they need to get their money and status right. They also realize they need to hit the gym more. As adults their

74

perception is that they are okay with women as long as they have their money, cars, and status. Some may even feel they are Mr. Goodbar until they lose their money and status. There is no organized subculture of Masked Men but rather several social networks and groups like fraternities where men with money and status will gather. The Masked Man will tend to see women more as trophies to go along with their other possessions.

Let me say this. Women who are average in looks and personality are seriously delusional thinking a man with money will want them. Average women have a better chance with a Goodbar who has a sex addiction.

Gamesmen for the most part weren't the cute boys or the smart boys who would grow up to be doctors, lawyers, or businessmen. Gamesmen see the writing on the wall from an early age and learn to make their own opportunities with women. They develop some type of game. They are some more organized sexual subcultures where Gamesmen will interact with each other, primarily on the Internet. A couple that come to mind are the Pick-Up Artist (PUA) community on the Internet that caters primarily to middle class white males. There is the smaller Macking community, also on the Internet that caters primarily to Black men. The differences in these two subcultures are interesting. The PUA community focuses more on routines and techniques to stimulate attraction in women. The Macking community focuses more into turning men into Masked Men. Outside the Internet there is a long tradition of Street Gamesmen primarily in lower income environments. These men, who go across racial lines, have developed a style of approaching and talking to women who are out in public. There has been some controversy with the Street Gamesmen lately because of efforts to criminalize "street harassment." That's a whole other blog. Indeed that's a town hall meeting broadcast on national TV.

One thing with the Gamesmen is that he can't sit back and wait for women to approach him because he is not a pretty boy with six pack abs. He's not pushing a Mercedes E-class and wearing tailored clothing. The Gamesman knows one simple thing: if he isn't aggressive, he sees no parts of the pussy. You can tell him women will come to him or that he needs to get a degree but that's not his reality.

The Nice Guy in middle and high schools was the regular guy. He wasn't popular. He didn't play sports. He wasn't the local drug runner. He didn't know how to approach women. These are the men who go through high school without a girlfriend and hang out with other clueless men. If they have a girlfriend it's someone they met through their social circles or lived in the neighborhood. If they go to college they fare a little better with girls who don't register with the top tier jocks and frat boys. Even then they may not get the relationships they want. Many will go on the Internet and get exposed to a Gamesmen subculture and still have problems. The Gamesmen subcultures are based on being aggressive and the Nice Guys typically don't have that.

What has happened is that there has developed several Nice Guy subcultures such as Men Going Their Own Way (MGTOW), Going Ghost (Black men withdrawing from the sexual landscape), Incel (Involuntarily Celibate), and TFL (True Forced Loneliness). There's are actually so many it would take a blog to deal with them all. I predict that unless something drastic happens these Nice Guy subcultures will become as mainstream as the LGBT community. I predict this will happen in the next five years. Again these are groups based on a shared perception of reality.

I could go on in talking about these subcultures. The bottom line is we are going to have to get deeper in relationship discussions. If you have 20 people coming together at someone's home discussing relationships there will not be consensus especially if the group is racially mixed. A Black women may say there there's a shortage of good Black men but she is only using that as a rationalization to go after white men. A white woman at the same time may say well there's a shortage of good white men but a look at her ankle will show a Queen of Spades tattoo. The Masked Man will say there's a shortage of good woman but because all he sees are overweight women and not magazine models. The Gamesman is wondering why women are trying to criminalize him approaching them on the street when they complain publicly about men not approaching them. The Nice Guy is wondering why he is there to begin with since he's being ignored. Mr. Goodbar is coming back from bedroom where a woman he just met gave him a blowjob.   See where I'm going with this?

We're going to have to go deeper.

Big Man Swag

November 30, 2014

Let me tell you something. I know I talk a lot about Mr. Goodbar, that fine dude that has all the ladies swooning. He is typically a handsome man with a muscular body. Some Goodbar types are tall and slim. Even people who follow the Alpha Male paradigm will say that the dominant men are tall and good-looking. Okay, fair enough. Life though isn't nice and neat like that. No matter if someone is using the select/non-select model I use in my writings or the more popular Alpha/Beta model there are always exceptions to the rule. The models are just guidelines that should not be considered absolute.   In plain language there are exceptions to the rule.

One exception that comes to mind are the Big Men. I'm talking about those cats who are not necessarily muscular or even that tall in many cases.   I'm talking about those big, hamburger and fries, rack of ribs, potato salad, and biscuit eating dudes.   Y'all know what I'm talking about.   Those men who eat their cereal with a big cake mixing bowl and a ladle.   Those cats who will go into a restaurant, sit down, look at the menu, call over the waiter and say, "I want page 2."

"You want something on page 2, sir."

"You ain't hearing me.   I want everything on the page."

I'm talking about those types of dudes who you know got a big ass outdoor grill somewhere.   A Big Man and a grill is as American as apple pie.   You know they got some ribs on, barbecuing during the winter and whatnot.

See I'm not going to say fat.   Some dudes are just naturally big.   They lose some weight and people will think they have a virus.   Some men just know how to carry their weight.   So why am I talking about Big Men?   Big Men be getting some bad ass women.

I've known a lot of Big Men in my day. Truth be told if I don't work out my weight can get up.   I've weighed as much as 270 in my life and still had women flirting with me. Even now, weighing 205, I'm only a month of eating pasta away from having to shop at a Big and Tall Men's shop. A co-worker on my day job calls me "Rom Diesel."

Yeah I've personally talked to thousands of women about their preferences. Now many will say that they want a tall, athletic type of man. Thing is that is more of an ideal. Like many men will say they want a woman with an hourglass figure. Very few men actually end up with that woman. It's the same thing with women. They can say they want a 6'2", handsome and muscular guy, who a stylish dresser, and has a six figure income. Realistically the best they can do is a 5'9" pudgy dude who is fashion challenged and makes a dollar more than minimum wage. Women are more pragmatic than many men realize. They will take what they can get. At the same time there are women who have a preference for Big Men.

Now I know that's hard for some people to believe. If you look at the pictures of men considered to be sexy on social media and the comments by women you would think that only the muscular men are physically attractive. Naw. There are two things happening. One, even though women are freer to express their preferences there is still a stigma for a woman to say she likes a particular physical type. It's the whole "look don't matter to women" myth that ironically mostly men promote. The second thing is that even in private women are influenced by their peers. So if a group of women are swooning over a tall muscular dude, one woman in the group may stay quiet because she's checking out the tall guy's chubby friend.

Now this isn't speculation on my part. I only talk about things I either have experienced personally or know someone whose word I trust has experienced personally. I've personally known a few dozen Big Men who had some fine women. There this one cat I'll call Big Tom. This dude even with constant exercise is still seen as burly. Despite his size he's still very athletic and an overall good person. He wasn't a player but he also didn't mess with no ugly women. Three of the women I knew he had sex with were Dimes. I knew because I knew the women. They told me. Yeah women tell me a lot of their personal business. Anyway I've known several men like this. These Big Men were not just getting women but fine women.

I actually know why they were getting these women but to explain would take a series of blogs because in order to explain one thing I would have to explain another. If there is an interest I may do a teleconference on the subject.

I will say this though. There were certain traits that these man had in common. One of the most important traits these men have is that they are down to earth. They are just some cool ass muthafuckas. There are typically not arrogant and are very approachable. I would say they are very gregarious. The average Big Man can damn near be anybody's friend. See the thing with Big Men is that they accept people as they are. No matter how crazy, ugly, obnoxious a person can be the Big Man can at least tolerate them. People tend to like people who can tolerate their bullshit. Big Men can tolerate a lot of things. Not to say they are pushovers. There is a point where a Big Man can be pushed too far and that's usually when they become extremely dangerous. I remember seeing a video of a small boy bullying a much bigger husky boy. The small boy kept hitting the husky boy until the husky boy got tired, picked up the small boy, and body slammed his ass.

Another thing with Big Men is that many have a depth to them that attracts women like flies to honey. Most women pick a man based on his outer appearance which usually means well-dressed, tall, handsome, and muscular. Then when a woman gets to know the man they are turned off. They'll say, "He was alright until he opened his mouth." An observation I've made is that many pretty boys will get one-night stands be it intercourse or a blow-job but not a second chance. Other than not being good in bed many lack any real substance. In other words, beyond outer appearance the women didn't find them interesting.

Now let's take the Big Men. A woman will be introduced to a man who could stand to lose 50 pounds. Her first instinct is to put him in the non-select category. They start to talk and the Big Man will have her laughing, she'll find out he's educated, and a business owner. If they are at a dance club she may find out he's a great dancer. If she gets comfortable enough with him she will have sex and the Big Man will rock her world. Especially if instead of that jackhammer sex, he grinds her by putting his weight on the right spot.

Fellas get that grind game together. Trust me. She'll thank you.

The substance piece is one thing. Some Big Men get chosen on the spot. We've all seen that overweight cat that has wicked swag. Those Big Men will have that fresh taper going with some designer glasses. They'll get that fitted shirt with a neck tie and sweater to match. They throw on those flat front pants with some Italian shoes. On top of that they have on the right amount of cologne. Even a woman who normally doesn't go for Big Men will get wet on the spot.

The thing with the Big Man is they accept themselves. They typically have been big all their lives. To be clear some will develop psychological issues such as depression. Some though, just accept who they are and go on live life to the fullest. They gonna eat, drink, and be merry. They will confidently walk up to pretty woman with a phat ass and whisper in her ear, "Girl you a big fine woman, won't you back that thing up." Big Men are bold dudes for real. Yeah, food, women, and laughter that's their thing.

Peace. And for the ladies: hug a Big Man today. You know you want to.

Different Women,
Different Alpha Males

January 11, 2015

One thing I see on the Internet and is talked about a lot with different groups of men is the concept of the Alpha Male. The Alpha Male is the tall, muscular, dominant man that gets most of the women. Though the racial aspect is rarely talked about in western culture the model for the Alpha Male is a heroic looking white man who looks like a comic book superhero or in real terms, the pro-football quarterback. New England Patriots quarterback Tom Brady is the icon for an Alpha Male. Even Men of other races must come close to this ideal to truly be considered Alpha Males. At least that is the prevailing idea if you read between the lines of those who promote the Alpha Male paradigm.

A big problem with many men in western culture is that the average man doesn't look like Tom Brady.   So you have whole groups of men trying to get around the standard Alpha Male paradigm such as the PUAs and Macks who in essence try to emulate what they think are Alpha Male traits since they typically don't have the physical package.   Then you have men like MGTOWs who basically just drop out of the game.

I want weigh in on this whole Alpha thing.   I think it's all bullshit.   In the past I have used the term "Alpha Male" more as a reference point and in some cases a sales tool.   Many men who have read and commented on my work have said that I promote Alpha Male ideals more so than Player/Pick-up ideals.   I went with it because no matter what I write different people will interpret my work according to their own level of understanding.   Really though my thoughts have always been that the prevailing definition of "alpha" has been limited and quite frankly a result of cultural chauvinism.   I've met several women who reject the popular image of the Alpha Male.

Let me share an observation I've made over my fifty years of life.   First of all women do indeed go for Alpha Males.   The thing is that in a diverse group of women each one will have a different definition of who is an Alpha Male. Their definition will be colored by their racial background, their socio-economic background, and their religious/spiritual beliefs.   Also their underlying gender orientation will affect their view of what constitutes an Alpha.   For example a woman who is heterosexual but has a lot of masculine energy may not find a tall, dominant man to be attractive because their energy will clash.   A short cooperative man may turn her on more.   Here's the game:

A woman's idea of an Alpha Male will tend to be a reflection of who she is as a person.

Let me provide some real world examples.   Names and small details have been changed to protect identities.

Jolynne is a white bisexual female in her late twenties from a solid middle class background.   She is very physically attractive as most men who have commented to me about her rate her as a Nine.   Though she easily attracts "Tom Brady" types she has a visceral hatred for men she derides as "Pretty Boys."   She gets hot for men who others would see as sensitive creative beta types.   Her choices are shaped by her sexual orientation, her vocation as a creative person (she crafts and sells products) and her spiritual beliefs which can be described as New Age.

Stephanie is a white female in her late forties from a poor dysfunctional background.   Though her lifestyle is solidly middle class now, her relationship choices were shaped during her childhood.   Most men would rate her an Eight and she would be seen as a MILF.   Though she gets plenty of attention from tall, rich, and dominant white men, they barely register on her radar.   Her idea of an Alpha Male is a younger man with long hair, visible tattoos, and piercings.

The scruffier the man looks the better. Her choices are shaped by her background and her underlying personality. Though she looks conservative on the surface she has several concealed tattoos and piercings.

Christine is a young Black female in her twenties from a middle class background. Most men would rate her as a Ten or as called in urban environments, a Dime. She literally looks a Black Barbie doll as she never wears pants and routinely wears tight sweaters, skirts, fishnets, and five inch heels. On the surface she would seem like she would be the type to be attracted to the standard Alpha Male, particularly a Black Masked Man. A man would not get the time of day from her unless he was heavily immersed in Black Christian church culture. An Alpha Male for her would be a man who has an important position in a church hierarchy. He also couldn't have tattoos and must have an overall conservative look. Her ideal man would be seen by most other women as a Nice Guy.

Jaclyn is a young Black female in her twenties from a middle class background. Most men would rate her as an Eight. She is very serious minded and focused on getting her education. In the Black community there is a prevailing notion that many young women want thugs. Jaclyn because of her goals and overall personality would not give a thug the time of day. To get her interested a man needs to have a somewhat conservative look and focused on getting his education. Her ideal man would be considered corny by many women.

These are just four small examples. The bottom line is that despite what many men think women have different versions of what constitutes an Alpha Male. Every single man is a Mr. Goodbar to some woman. In my work I really don't encourage men to be Alpha Males though I certainly come off that way. If one reads my work carefully they will see that I promote more a man developing himself to be the best he can be.

See the real problem with the prevailing Alpha Male paradigm is that it sets an impossible ideal. Most men aren't going to be 6'2". Their genetics prevent this. A man can lift all he wants but will still never be cut and defined. A man's muscularity is determined by his genetics. A man may not have dominant personality in that he is the center of attention in a crowd. Let me really get into this last one.

Many seduction gurus teach men how to be more social and outgoing. They teach men how to be the center of attention. Being the center of attention is not always the best way to get a woman. Many women prefer quiet low key men. Using myself as an example I'm more of an introvert. I've never been the life of the party type of man. Now I'm not nervous standing in front of a group of people and I'm actually quite comfortable doing so. Being introverted means I'm comfortable staying to myself. Many women are turned on by that strong silent type.

Also a man's particular mission in life may require that he doesn't draw a lot of attention to himself. I remember a conversation I had with a co-worker on my day job a few days ago. He is a naturally a laid back type of dude. We were talking about secret agents and he was surprised that I told him he would be a great secret agent because he doesn't attract attention to himself and thus would be able to move around easily. In real life, undercover operatives for intelligence and law enforcement agencies don't look like they do in the movies. A tall, blond haired muscular man would be too identifiable to make an effective undercover operative. He would stand out too much. Undercovers have to be able to blend into the background. Also jobs like an airplane pilot or heart surgeon require a man to have a calm nature. Gregarious people are not necessarily good at stressful situations.

My advice to any man reading is stop trying to be something that you are not. Push that whole Alpha Male paradigm out of your mind. Many men are stressing themselves out when they don't need to. Women have different tastes. The smartest thing any man can do is build up his talents to fulfill his personal life mission. While doing this he needs to pay attention to see which women like what he is doing. It might be one hundred women or it might be five. It is better for a man to focus on the five women who find him attractive and not to try to change himself for the women who don't see him. It's so much they don't see him as it is that they are looking for their own personal Alphas.

Raw Game: The Look

February 15, 2015

My fiftieth birthday was this past Friday the 13th. Hey it's a lucky day for me. I'm in a great mood. Fifty years of life. Fifty years of kicking ass. I look back at my life and quite frankly don't have any regrets. I've done a lot. My next fifty will be even better as I rise and transform to a new level. Since I'm in a good mood I going to share some real game with my readers. I know I said I wouldn't teach game even though I drop gems every now and then but I'm feeling generous. For my birthday I gave my sons what they wanted. So I took them to Chuck E. Cheese and bought them some game cartridges and some Legos. I'm going to give my readers some raw game.

I know that's what most of y'all come to my blog for anyway. So let's get right into it.

Many people are of the mindset that someone has to look good to attract women. I'm of that mindset and emphasize working on one's physical appearance. The thing is most people think looks are about good genetics. Many men feel like they have to be over six feet with bulging muscles and a movie star face. A man having those things is always going to get some attention but the game is deeper than that. Way deeper. There are many who have those classic features and yet either end up with average looking women or are lacking in female companionship period. Many will wonder why women are not falling all over them. Allow me to explain.

Women in their DNA will always have an optimal physical type they are attracted to. It might be a muscular man, a tall man, or a stocky man. That's the deep primal level of attraction. Here's the game though. A woman can run into a man who represents her optimal DNA attraction and still not feel the all-important vagina tingle. Indeed she might even be turned off by her optimal match. Why is this?

As I've written before there are two major schools of thought with regard to getting women. Check that, I should say beautiful women. Men are not reading blogs and spending money just to get the Plain Jane or homely woman who might actually want them. The whole men's dating advice industry is about getting hot women. One major school of thought is that as long as a man has looks, money, and status (LMS), he can get beautiful women. The other school of thought is that a man needs to have good Game to get beautiful women. Both have their limitations. The LMS School is focused on mainstream definitions of good looks, money, and status. The icon for the LMS School is a tall, clean cut, white male who is an upper middle class professional. Even men of other racial backgrounds must come close to that standard. For example a Black man following that school will typically be clean shaven with a conservative haircut. The problem with this school is that most men will not have the genetics and the background to thrive with LMS.

The Game School is for the men who know they don't fit the square jawed moneyed model of LMS. So those who follow the Game School will scheme. They work to figure out strategies to get with beautiful women using any means necessary. This includes using everything from pick-up lines, to faking what they believe to be Alpha Male behavior, to outright lies. The more successful Gamesmen really don't do well with beautiful women and most of their "conquests" are with average women. The reality is that Game as it is taught is failing the overwhelming majority of men. There are many who see Game as it is taught as a scam.

Now someone is probably wondering which school I teach from. Neither. My school of thought is the Sexy Man

School. A careful reading of my books and blogs will show my focus is more on a man developing sexual charisma. A man with sexual charisma will get approached by beautiful women. He can be an unemployed man living in his mom's basement and still get more and better quality women than a LMS man. Whereas a Gamesman has to approach and talk to a woman, a sexy man can be quiet and shy and still have women all over him.

One more thing, let me clarify my use of the word "Game" in the context of this blog. When the word "Game" is used by dating coaches it usually means techniques to seduce beautiful women. Keep in mind that these are primarily white male coaches. I use the term "Game" in the context it is used in Black, urban, environments which actually has several meanings but boils down to basic "knowledge and common sense." Now that I will teach and have been teaching. So let's get into Game about "the look."

Women choose men based on their look. So many men believe that look is based on raw genetics. They believe that since they don't have a model face and are of average height that beautiful women will not give them the time of day. They are wrong. Yes as I pointed out earlier women do have a physical type they find attractive but that is only the foundation. There are many layers to a man's look that will turn a woman on sexually. Here's the game: Women view men through their own **SUBCULTURAL** lens. I'm going to use an example from the Black community to illustrate my point. To be clear what I'm about to write applies to any racial or ethnic group.

So you have Black man we'll call Kelvin. He looks like a Black Ken doll. Kelvin is 6'2" with a square jaw, aquiline nose, and short curly hair brushed into waves. He has a light brown skin complexion. In the Black community he would be called a "pretty boy." He has a muscular body build. He is educated, speaks well, and wears tailored suits. He drives a late model luxury car. Kelvin is from an old money family. In addition he is a doctor. According to all of this he should be the man with Black women. The reality is that he is seen as sexually attractive to only a small percentage of Black women. Why is this?

Here's some raw game. Many non-Blacks and indeed many Blacks see Black America as one large monolithic entity. The reality is that there are **FOUR** Black Americas, which when broken down can effectively be divided into well over a **HUNDRED** distinct subcultures. The same can be said for white America, Asian America, and Hispanic America. A man's looks are filtered through a woman's subcultural lens. In other words what a woman finds attractive will depend on her particular subculture. We'll take Kelvin through a scenario where he encounters women from each of the four Black Americas.

Kelvin at a mixer for Black professionals. He stands out only slightly looks wise in the crowd because the other men are in shape and have tailored suits on as well. He meets a slender Black woman named Shelly who quite frankly

95

looks like a Black Barbie. She is also an executive with a large corporation. Her background is similar to Kelvin's. They both grew up in **"Upper Class" Black America**. These are the folks described in Lawrence Otis Graham's book, "Our Kind of People." In Shelly's eyes Kelvin is drop dead handsome and more importantly fits into her cultural paradigm. Indeed Kelvin does well with women in Upper Class Black America even if they are not in his immediate social circle. There are issues when Kelvin deals with women from the other Black Americas.

Kelvin is a doctor. As such he encounters many Black women who work as nurses. They don't look like the Black Barbies he encounters at Upper Class events. The Black nurses he encounters tend to be plainer in facial features, with more weight on their frames. They are still above average in attraction. Sevens as opposed to Nines. The women are representatives of **"Mainstream" Black America**. Mainstream Black America is more working class and lower end professionals. The values tend to be more socially conservative with Christian church membership and family values more emphasized. The Black nurses see Kelvin as attractive in a physical way but they are otherwise turned off by him. They see him as a bourgie pretty boy who comes off as being too good to go out with any of them. In other words he doesn't **LOOK** like he is down to Earth. He doesn't **LOOK** like the type who on a Sunday would go to a loud Baptist church service in the morning and then to a backyard barbecue in the afternoon where "Uncle Junior and them" are playing spades. When a woman looks at a man she isn't just looking at his face and listening to his words. She's looking at him wondering if he can hang out with her. Kelvin's physical good looks were irrelevant in this regard. His money and status actually works against him with women in this group.

Kelvin is out driving through a poor neighborhood on the way to a charity event. He stops at a gas station. The attendant is a young Black woman named L'Aquila. She is very physically attractive with a pretty face and slim but curvy body. She looks like a ghetto version of Barbie. She also has a hair weave and several visible tattoos. If L'Aquila was a gold digger she would be turned on by Kelvin because not only was he cute but he dressed like he had money and his car was nice. L'Aquila didn't think much about Kelvin because she didn't look to men for money. Growing up with a single mother she learned early in life not to depend on men for anything. L'Aquila had her own hustles going which included being a part of a shoplifting crew. Her gas station job was a cover. L'Aquila is representative of **"Underclass" Black America.** Unfortunately when outsiders think of Black America they see the face of the underclass. The reality is that the largest Black America is the church going, hardworking, Mainstream group. The thing with the Underclass is that there is a pervading sense of survival by any means necessary. This is where criminal activity is a way of life. This is where you find several generations of a family on welfare. Even those who do work in the underclass tend to have low pay jobs with no future.   Unless an underclass woman is practicing some form of sex work, Kelvin wouldn't register greatly on their radar.   In the urban environment being a pretty boy can be hazardous because they are seen as soft.   The men who win out are the true thugs.   An underclass woman is looking for a man who looks like he can protect her and also bang the hell out of her.   A square jaw mean nothing if the owner **LOOKS** like he can't fight. Money and status does play a role within the community in that the top level hustler gets attention.   The Game that dating coaches teach is absolutely useless with underclass women.   You have to very direct with underclass women. Bottom line is that underclass women wouldn't find Kelvin attractive because he doesn't **LOOK** like he is "about that life."

Kelvin gets to the event.   It is sponsored by a Pan-African group raising money for an independent school.   He was invited by a medical school classmate who is also a Pan-Africanist.   Kelvin in his tailored suit is very out of place in this environment.   Even though people at the event listened politely to Kelvin's presentation he felt some tension.   The people at the event were representative of what I'll call **"Alternative" Black America.**   A major difference between the Alternatives and the other three is religion.   The dominant religion in the other Black Americas is Christianity. In Alternative Black America the major religions will tend to be Black Islam, Kemetic paths, and Traditional African Religion. Also there are many philosophical schools of

98

thought such as Pan-Africanism, Afrocentrism, Black Nationalism, and RBG. There is also a strong aesthetic sensibility to Alternative Black America. Kelvin looks like a brown white man with his jaw and nose. He is supremely attractive to Upper Class Black women and at least good looking to Mainstream and Underclass women. He doesn't register on the radar of most Alternative Black women. Western culture holds up the white male and female as the apex of human attraction. Any sensible culture holds up its own as the most attractive. In Western culture, the Black people that other Black people hold up as attractive tend to come closer to the white ideal. Alternative Black America holds up Black physical features as most ideal. The Alternative ideal is Black men and women with distinctly African features and natural hair. Most Alternative women will wear their hair chemical and weave free. Many men will wear locs. Being called "African" may be seen as an insult with people from the other Black Americas and a great compliment to Alternatives. Kelvin's **LOOKS** aren't attractive to Alternative women. Neither is his money and status. For "Game" to have any impact Kelvin would have to be able to speak the same subcultural language as the Alternatives.

I know this blog has been long but the raw game, is deep. It's not something to be learned from a book, or a weekend seminar. The raw game is life. So many men are caught up into just trying to improve their looks, money, and status. That may work in mainstream terms regardless of race but it is also limiting. What's happening in the world is that the mainstreams of any culture are shrinking. More and more people are asserting their identities and finding like-minded people to form communities. A man can use plastic surgery improve his looks. He can make more money and upgrade his status. There is still going to be women who don't like his looks and don't care about his money and status. Game is irrelevant for man trying to use it on a woman from a different subculture.

Here's the takeaway from this blog. When men see a woman they really don't think much beyond her face and body. Many men find out the hard way that a toxic personality is attached to that pretty face. Women though will look at a man's face and body as well. They will also try ascertain his social class, economic status, religion, and general philosophy in life. To do so they will check out how he is dressed particularly his shoes, they will check for visible tattoos, haircuts, and even if he has a watch. They will make an assessment in 30 seconds or less and place the man in the select and non-select categories before the man opens his mouth to spit "Game." A man's look is very important because it is a non-verbal communication to a woman.

It isn't so much looks matter as it is "The Look" the matters.

There is No Spoon

March 22, 2015

"Do not try and bend the spoon. That's impossible. Instead... only try to realize the truth."
"What truth?"
"There is no spoon."
"There is no spoon?"
"Then you'll see, that it is not the spoon that bends, it is only yourself."
-The Matrix

    The above is a piece of dialogue from a classic movie, "The Matrix." I find it interesting that this movie has influenced so many people. I'm not going to go into the numerous ways but for the purposes of this blog I will go into two of the concepts. The first is the concept of a matrix. A matrix in general is a system. Applied to relationships people use the term "matrix" to refer to the common expectations for male/female relationships in Western, particular American culture. Many men who leave American society to find cooperative women for sex and marriage will say they are "escaping the matrix." That's one concept from the movie. The second more prevalent concept is that of taking the "red pill."

In one of many classic scenes in "The Matrix," the mentor character, Morpheus, offers the hero, Neo, a choice between two pills, a red pill and a blue pill. If Neo takes the red pill, he will learn the true nature of the matrix. If he takes the blue pill he goes back to being a pawn of the system. Of course Neo takes the red pill and thus we have a trilogy, animated features, and online games. "Red pill" has become a part of our cultural lexicon.

Yeah...

There are whole subcultures of men on the Internet who call themselves "Red Pill" because they believe they know the truth of male/female interactions. Many of these men are former Nice Guys who were raised to believe that as long as they worked hard and stayed out of trouble they would be rewarded with the love and affection of a beautiful woman. That's until they are friendzoned for the umpteenth time or the object of their desires gets pregnant by the village idiot. These men were also raised to believe that a man's physical appearance didn't matter. Their world is shattered when a broke pretty boy has women stalking him. "Red Pill" generally means that a man sees the realities of women.

Before I go further let me share a bias I have. I will probably offend some people with what I'm about to say but I have to keep it raw. Many of these men calling themselves

"Red Pill" are white and middle class. Even non-white men who identify themselves as "Red Pill" tend to have a white male, middle class orientation as they would be called "Oreos" if Black, "Bananas" if Asian, and "Coconuts" if Hispanic. Black men who grew up in underclass environments are "red pilled" from the time they start playing with kids outside of their homes. Same thing with white men who grew up in poor environments. People in poor environments can't afford to go through life with blinders on. Men from solid middle class backgrounds grew up sheltered to a significant extent though they may believe otherwise. When grown men talk about they are "red pill" because they find out that looks matter or that a woman may want a man just for sex, I roll my eyes. Stuff many men are calling "red pill" is stuff I knew before my tenth birthday in **1975**. I was an adult before I realized that many men didn't have knowledge that I considered common sense. At the same time I have been working on my patience with such men because everybody has different life experiences. Thing is the "red pill" concept is deeper than knowing that women got hot off of looks.

I consider very few men as "red pill." Let me explain why I say that. In "The Matrix" Neo not only took the red pill but went through a transformation. He went from a computer programmer to someone who could fly and stop bullets with a thought. Even other characters were able to do fantastic things because they had taken the "red pill." An old adage is "knowledge is power." Okay, so Red Pill Men have knowledge, so now what? Most of these men see how things really are in male/female interactions and yet they do nothing but complain. They will say, "Women want alpha males," "women want bad boys," "women want tall men," so on and so forth. From where I sit men get a little bit of insight and then go on the Internet and complain. Many men will stop interacting with women, while others will try to get women to change their behavior. One subculture of men will learn "game" in order to get the women they desire. To me they are still not truly "red pill."

In "The Matrix" Neo had the ability to mold the matrix to his liking. He was able to bend and break the rules when it suited him. Thus he was able to stop bullets and to fly. In terms of relationships if a man was truly "red pill" he would not only have knowledge of sexual realities but he would have the ability to bend those realities to his needs. For example, many Red Pill Men say that women only care about looks, money, and status. Yet there are ugly, broke men who have a harem of women. Other red pill men may say that it takes "game" to get women. Yet there are average looking men who don't use game and yet will consistently get attractive girlfriends. No matter what a general "rule" is, there is always exceptions. The man who truly has taken the red pill is the exception. The key to being an exception is perception.

I quoted the spoon scene at the start of this blog. In the scene Neo saw the boy bending the spoon. That was his initial perception. By realizing that in the world of the

Matrix everything is an illusion, Neo simply changed his perception and thus was able to bend the spoon. Most men whether they call themselves "red pill," or just regular guys are stuck in seeing things from a certain way. This is through no fault of their own. Most people will go from birth to death with the same general perception. Once people develop a certain perspective it takes a whole lot for them to change it. Let me use an example.

A man will perceive that it takes looks, money, and status to get an attractive woman. In this way he develops a belief system. This man will **ONLY** perceive that which **SUPPORTS** his beliefs. He **BELIEVES** that it takes looks, money, and status to get women. His mind will only register instances where his belief is supported. No matter where he goes he will only see beautiful women dealing with good-looking men with money. Now another man believes that beautiful women only like bad boys or thugs. No matter where he goes he will only see beautiful women with thugs. Still a third man believes attractive women only deal with men who are 6'2". This man will only see instances where this belief is supported. Now when these same men encounter situations that goes against their beliefs, they will either tell themselves that something is wrong with the situation or go as far as to forget that they saw anything. Many men stay with their perceptions even when presented with something that contradicts their beliefs.

The true "red pill" man knows that "there is no spoon." Most men either see women going for a certain type of man or they try to "bend" the women into finding them attractive. Most dating advice is geared towards changing the woman even in cases where a man is advised to change something within himself. These men are trying to "bend the spoon." The key though is simply changing the perception. The way to do this is to see the big picture.

One thing I've picked up from observing different subcultures of men and their interactions with women is that most stay stuck in one mode of perception. The key is to see **EVERYTHING**. Not only must a man have the ability to see everything but have the wisdom to accept the knowledge. A man can see a beautiful woman going for a tall good looking man. The same man if he keeps his eyes open can see a woman going for a short average looking man. It's not an issue if it's a common sight but rather that it happens. A man can see a beautiful woman hanging out with a thug. If his perception is open he can also see an equally beautiful woman hanging out with a clean cut nerd. Once a man expands his perception he can see the greater possibilities.

Let me share some things about myself because I don't talk theory. I've gone on record as saying I've dated several hundred women in my fifty years of life. What I'm about to share I've never said publicly. Consider it a specific weapon of mass seduction in my arsenal. Out of these hundreds of women I can count the number of women on one hand who have called me "good-looking." I've had only one woman out of several hundred say I was her type. A significant number of women I've dated I started out with on rocky terms. By the terms I use in my books and blogs I wasn't select. At least not on the surface. My secret weapon was my belief in myself. My thought was that if I could have a 30 minute conversation with any woman she could find me **INTERESTING.** My secret was knowing that **NOTHING** is absolute. I don't adhere to the so-called rules. Reality is malleable and I bend it to my pleasure. A woman can want whatever, it doesn't have anything to do with what I bring to the table.

Too many focus on the spoon. By realizing that there is no spoon they will see that what they thought was reality around them was nothing but an illusion. When a man can cut through the illusion and find the success he wants with women then he is truly "red pill."

Leave Basic Women Alone

April 19, 2015

I remember years when I was a teenager. I was walking in my neighborhood. I was going to visit some young girl. Keep in mind I'm not walking through an alley. I'm walking down a residential street of well-kept row houses in a clean middle class area. As I was walking a rat came running along at a leisurely pace. Right out there on the sidewalk. He started keeping pace with me. Now I wasn't scared. When I lived in a poor neighborhood in Anacostia, Washington, DC we had rats and mice so bad that we started to name them. Anyway as we were walking the rat decided he wanted to have a conversation with me.

Rat: Hey man what's up?

Rom: Nothing special. Just walking over to this girl's house.

Rat: Yeah, I'm going over to this girl's house too. Gonna make me a litter. You?

Rom: Naw rat, I gonna wrap it up.

Rat: Yeah I guess you need to. Humans take so long to have a baby.

Rom: True, true.

Rat: So how come you not scared of me? Most humans run while I'm out.

Rom: Dealt with some of your cousins out in Anacostia. I leave y'all alone, y'all leave me alone. I know rats ain't scared of people.

Rat: True, true. We just get out of people's way because it's easier. You all right man what's your name?

Rom: Rommy.

Rat: Oh shit! Rommyo?

Rom: Yeah some people call me that too.

Rat: I heard some human females mention your name here and there. You a cool bamma. I was thinking about biting you too. Wait till I tell the fellas. I met the infamous Rommyo."

Rom: I guess I should be flattered.

Rat: Yeah you got a rep. Hey I'm about to turn down this alley. Let me know if I can do anything for you.

Rom: You and your cousins can stay off my street.

Rat: Where you live?

Rom: Over there on 6th Street.

Rat: I know where that is. I'll tell my rats to stay from over there. You still might have to deal with that rat Lou. Lou and them crazy. They don't listen to me. Take it easy Rommyo.

Rom: Hey you too.

✳✳✳✳✳✳✳✳✳✳✳✳✳

This convo actually took place. If Richard Pryor can talk to animals so can I. My point with sharing with this incident was that I didn't have trouble from this rat because I left it alone. So what does this have to do with the subject of this blog? Very simple, men need to leave Basic Women alone. So what do I mean when I say Basic Women? When say Basic women I don't mean Plain Janes or even ugly, overweight women. I mean women who really don't have anything going for them. For me a basic woman can be a Plain Jane. She can also a ratchet with several tattoos and a weave down to her ass. Basic to me is the opposite of the Quality Woman that most men want. Who is that Quality Woman?

If there is one common type of woman that all men want regardless of their race, nationality, or economic class it is the Quality Woman. This woman is first of all is physically attractive. Now different cultures have different standards of physical beauty. Some cultures prefer slimmer women while others prefer more voluptuous women. The common denominator is a woman having a shapely figure regardless of her actual size. In other words there is no culture on the planet that sees a fat stomach as sexually appealing. Subcultures yes, major cultures no. Indeed, many so-called chubby chasers are just men who can't get swimsuit models. Many men pick what's available and not what they actually want.

The Quality Woman is more than a physical package. The Quality Woman is plain likeable beyond her looks. In a time where many women complain about a shortage of good men the Quality Woman will have several men as at least associates if not friends. Someone cynical may say that these men are just beta orbiters who are waiting for a chance with a beautiful woman, and that is indeed a factor. I would argue though that a Quality Woman is just cool like that. I've known and still know several very beautiful women who are just "good peoples." Sometimes a man is drawn to a woman for her physical beauty and gets to know her and realizes the compatibility isn't there for a relationship. He puts her in the friend zone. Contrary to popular belief there are heterosexual men out there who are not trying to have sex with every woman they encounter.

The most important factor with a Quality Woman is that she is comfortable with being a feminine woman. True femininity is not celebrated in this culture. A Tantra master once said that, "everywhere I go the men are men and so are the women." True femininity is ironically attacked more by Feminists than it is by men. Let me break down the real deal about Feminism. It has nothing to do with equality. It has everything to do with power. Feminists want power and associate power with doing things with a masculine energy. Masculine power is using force. Truly feminine women don't use force to get want they want. They use cooperation and a submissive nature. Many feminine women have been attacked by Feminists for this reason. Yet the feminine nature is actually more powerful because while the masculine energy has to use brute strength to accomplish its goals the feminine nature has things handed to it freely. Now that's power.   I'll get into this more in another blog.   My main point is that a Quality Woman is also a feminine woman.

Now before I get some inbox messages from people who will disagree with how I describe a Quality Woman keep in mind this is how heterosexual men see women.   When I categorize men into different groups it is according to how women see men and not how men see themselves.   Many men see themselves as select while in reality women see them as non-select.   Well it's the same thing as far as how men see women.   Many women see themselves as Quality Women while men see them as a hot mess.   Now this isn't simply about Quality Women.   I want to address a problem I see in society in general.   The problem is that too many men focus their attention on Basic Women.

I lurk on a lot of websites, blogs, and social media pages.   I'm also talking with men of all walks of life in the streets.   It's is truly hard to find something on the Internet or in the barbershop that is focused on the Quality Woman other than to say that there is a shortage.   Most of the media and the conversations, even the more positive ones focus on jacked up women.   The only time I can find more positive conversations is when the media page is woman-centered and the men on the page are simps kissing up to women in order to get some pussy.   The male-dominated pages tears into women.

I see a lot of pages talking about "thots."   For those who are not hip "thot" means "that hoe over there."   Some of these pages and websites will have memes, pictures, videos and even private tweets that point out the nature of thots. Even the pages that might not use that term will highlight the negative behavior of Basic Women. These pages and websites will have a lot of commentary from several followers. Real-life conversations are not really any different.

Whenever a group of men come together no matter the original purpose of the meeting the conversation turns to women. The conversation is very rarely about the positive qualities of women in general. Mention might be made of a woman here and there who can be described as a Quality Woman but for the most part the complaints are about Basic Women.

It's funny how women like to go on TV and on social media to complain about the shortage of good men but if someone were to talk to a large group of men they would find that many men feel that there is a shortage of good women. For their point of view there is a strong argument to say that. Now what I'm about to say is my own personal point of view. Usually what I write is from the perspective of the group. There have been things I've written in this blog that didn't represent my own feelings. Many cases I'm speaking for men who don't have the ability to communicate that I do. The following is my personal perspective. I'm sharing this because I believe it will help other men.

First thing I will honestly say is that the overwhelmingly majority of women who I have had in my life as lovers, friends, and associates have been Quality Women. I don't do basic. The FEW times I have dealt with Basic

Women was when they wore a very good mask and they were very persistent. Even then I can think of only a few times I've had sex with a Basic Woman. This happened when I was younger and less experienced. Most Basic Women don't register on my radar. In fact, most Basic Women keep their distance from me. Thing about Basic Women is that they have a certain type. Basic Women tend to go for men they can understand. They understand the man with the earrings, tattoos, and pants hanging off their ass. They understand the grown man who always wearing sports jerseys and sneakers when they are not playing a sport. Basic Women don't understand a man like me. Men like me get called lame because I dress and carry myself like the grown ass man that I am. I'm cool with that though because Quality Women are attracted to grown men. Women who label a man as lame or corny are little girls. That's some high school shit and I have zero tolerance for it from a thirty year-old woman. I want them to see me that way. Makes my job easier.

When I'm out and about I don't focus on ratchets. Like the rat I talked about earlier I just let them be. They can do whatever. I'm not going to start and maintain a social media page talking about ratchets. I'm not going to waste my energy. I focus solely on Quality Women. When I used to go parties, clubs, or anything where there was a lot of women I would zero in on the Quality Women and would usually walk away with a phone number or sometimes more. Sometimes they would focus on me. I remember I went to a birthday party back in the day. The male/female ratio was

114

interesting. It was about thirty people there. There were nine women there and twenty odd men. The least of the women there was an Eight. So there was a lot of competition for a few women. I was one of the winners. I was dancing most of the night with at least two women sandwiching me. I had one young woman who spent two songs rubbing her breasts against my back while I was grinding another woman's phat ass. I've always had very attractive women show me that type of love. I did so without using money, status, looks, or game. The key is the energy.

See I give very little energy to Basic Women. Anybody who knows me will tell you I say few negative things about women. Even in my blogs how much do I "bash" women? I might say something here and there but it will be very general. It's not that I don't see the negative behavior of many women. I see it just fine. Indeed I see better than most men. I made a choice though. I chose not to focus on the negative women. That diminishes my energy. I've had some very beautiful women who have wanted to have sex with me at the most and at least wanted to be a sincere friend to me at the least. I have been validated by women who were/are beautiful inside and out. Why would I do something stupid and focus on ugly ass Basic Women? I'm talking not only physically ugly but ugly personalities as well. Let's be raw, even the physically attractive thots and ratchets tend to have fucked-up personalities. So why are men focusing energy on that?

115

What I have done is simply focused on Quality Women. Just to be clear it hasn't always been about physical beauty. Truth be told I'm not moved by solely physical beauty. The thing moves me is a woman's personality, sensuality, and level of class. I've dealt with some Quality Women who looked like Plain Janes until I had conversations with them. A plain woman becomes beautiful once you see and feel her spirit.

So I have focused on Quality Women and I've discovered something very fascinating. I have found when someone focuses their energy enough on something they will find an abundance of whatever they are looking for. Many men find an abundance of Basic Women because that's what they focus on. Myself I focus on Quality Women. As a result I personally know an abundance of such women. Many men complain about slim pickings but I say they simply need to change their perceptions.

To the men reading this leave the Basic Women alone. Don't be so thirsty that you put up with any bullshit. The pussy does not have a cape hanging out of it. Pull away from the websites, blogs, and social media where the focus is on the negative behavior of Basic Women. Pull away from your social circle if the focus is too much on Basic Women. Shift your energy to Quality Women. The more you shift your focus the more you will find an abundance of the Quality Women you desire.

Lemonade

May 3, 2015

So in my last blog I talked about the Female Gaze and that women are free to choose a man based solely on physical appearance. Even though this shouldn't be news there are still many men in denial. A significant part of my books and blogs focus on improving physical appearance which I define as the overall look of a person. Even though I focus on the total package there are still many men who feel like they cannot get quality women because they are facially or height challenged. In the language of the streets they are homely or short, sometimes both. Many feel that no matter how much muscle they put on or how much they max out their credit cards at a high end men's store they will still be denied the caress of the attractive woman. Their reasoning is that no matter what they do they cannot control basic genetics. If they are homely or short there is nothing they can do about it. I agree with them.

If a man has a certain bone structure there is nothing he can do about it other than expensive plastic surgery. How many men got money like that though? A man can increase his height through surgery which is reportedly expensive and painful. Once again how many men got money like that? The reality is that if a man is homely or short he will pretty much have to deal with that the rest of his life. So does that mean he cannot get into a relationship with a quality woman? Hell to the no! I only write about what I know so let me use a couple of examples from real life of how a homely or short man can still get very attractive women.

Back in the late eighties I knew this guy I'll call Kevin. Even though I normally have a hard time judging another man's face this dude was ugly. He called himself ugly. The women in that particular social circle called him ugly. Now I knew two of the women he had relationships with. Both were certifiably beautiful. One had placed in a local beauty contest that was a feeder for a national beauty pageant. The other had been featured in a prominent local magazine as one of the most beautiful women in Washington, DC. I also saw him hugged up with a beautiful woman that looked like the beauty contestant. Now I know someone wants to know what type of game he ran to get these women. I'm not sure about two of them but the beauty contestant told me some things. We had dated a few times so she told me a LOT of things. Anyway she said Kevin was Thorough. He wasn't the most handsome brotha but he was confident in how in he moved through life. From knowing him he was very athletic with a slim but muscular build. He was serious minded and he didn't take any bullshit off anybody. He was a very cool person overall. He didn't walk around thinking that being homely would prevent him from living the life he wanted to live.

In the late nineties I met this brotha I'll call Jabbar. I'm still not entirely convinced that Jabbar wasn't the result of a government conspiracy to create a genetically engineered superman using reverse engineered technology from one of the crashed UFOs they say don't exist. Jabbar was a certified genius maybe even a prodigy. He was getting a doctorate in molecular biology when I met him. Dude was just flat out smart in other areas as well. On top of that he was a superior athlete. I played in a rec league football game with him one time. He pretty much dominated the game. He was also in top physical shape with defined muscles and normally dressed like a fashion model. Jabbar's haircut was always on point. He was a genius level, athletic, muscular, pretty boy with swag.

He was also 5'5", weighing in at 130 lbs. soaking wet with clothes on.

A lot of short guys will complain about their height and use that as an excuse as to why their lives are miserable and women don't want them. I never heard an excuse come from Jabbar's mouth. If he made a mistake or didn't know something he would simply say he made a mistake and didn't know something. He would immediately correct the mistake and take the time to educate himself on a particular subject. As far as women this dude didn't care. He was fearless about approaching the women he wanted. He didn't go for average women either. He was fond of tall, pretty women with killer bodies. He was unapologetic about it.

I really have a lot of examples. Yes women go for physical appearance but women will take other factors into consideration. The reality is that there are not enough 6'2" Adonis looking men with money and 10 inch dicks walking around. As I have written a few times women are way more pragmatic than men give them credit for. Let me share some raw game about women and how facially or height challenged men can still win. There are two general things a man must take into his consciousness with regard to this matter.

The first thing a man has to do is accept his physical self. There are some things that can be easily changed and some things that take a lot of money to change. A man cannot naturally change his facial bone structure or his height. This is embedded in his DNA. It was the hand he was dealt. He simply has to make the best of the situation. As far as the face he can make it look better with grooming. Simple things such a haircuts and good dental hygiene makes a great difference. Sometimes a man can enhance his look with glasses and facial hair. A man can't control his basic bone structure but he can control how it is presented. Also I emphasize hitting the gym. Weight loss especially makes a man's face look more chiseled and handsome.

As far as height there is nothing short of surgery that can do anything. Also from my observation and research from nearly 30 years of paying attention to such things the men who get the most women are rarely over 6 feet tall. Most Mr. Goodbars are under 6 feet tall. Tall Goodbars are rare. Explaining why that is the case will take a book because the explanation gets into a body of knowledge that isn't currently mainstream. The average height of a man who gets multiple women is about 5'8". I've met a whole lot of tall men who had trouble getting women. Even the tall men who get a lot of women tend to be Masked Men.

The second thing a man has to take into his consciousness is what women actually look for from a man. We get all these things about security and sex but at the deepest level these are not the things that women are looking to receive from a man. The thing a woman looks for from a man is to **FEEL** a certain way. A woman doesn't so much want to see a man or be with a man but they want to **FEEL** him. When a person drinks alcohol they are looking to be intoxicated by that alcohol. They want a certain buzz. When a woman eats chocolate they want to feel a certain way. They want to feel something in their entire being. Women look for what a mentor calls **Romantic Intoxication**. To simplify things I'll call it **Feel Good**.

It's hard for me as a man to adequately describe this feeling as I don't have a woman's hormones. I just know when a woman is on that Feel Good. Women get a certain glow when they are intoxicated. They typically call it "being in love." At its most basic level it's when a woman is in lust with a man. There's nothing rational about it. Indeed most women become addicted to this feeling. This is the reason why women chase certain men. Mr. Goodbar is distinguished from other men because he knows how to deliver the Feel Good. He's like a drug dealer hooking a new client. Once a woman is turned out by a Goodbar she has major problems trying to deal with a regular man. Indeed the common pattern for a woman is to have a sex with a Goodbar, get dumped by said Goodbar, talk trash about men, and then get another Goodbar. Masked Men win only by mimicking the overall aura of Mr. Goodbar. Mr. Goodbar has the pure product. The Masked Man has the watered down version.

Non-select men such as Gamesmen and Nice Guys fail with women for no other reason than they cannot deliver to the Feel Good. That's really the only difference between select and non-select men.

When a woman selects a man on physical appearance she is really looking for a man who **LOOKS** like he can deliver the Feel Good. This is not always the case. Many, many women have made the following statement to me in one form or another, "Rom, the guy looked right. Said all the right things. He is educated with money. That spark just wasn't there." The women in all of these cases were dealing with Masked Men. Yes, women go for physical appearance but experience teaches them that all that glitters isn't gold. Physical appearance should be seen as the lure and nothing more. Many men have a good lure and it's needed to attract women. A man still needs to deliver the product which is the Feel Good.

The man who is homely or short can win by learning how to deliver Feel Good. The first thing to understand is that a homely man has a distinct advantage over a pretty boy. See when women see a handsome man they get aroused not because of anything he did. The get aroused by the expectation that this Adonis has the Feel Good. The woman's imagination is what aroused her. Very few men can match the sex that the woman had in mind. For that reason many women end up disappointed because their expectations were not fulfilled.

When women meet homely men or short men or even overweight men there are no expectations. Women rarely have an initial attraction to these men. As a result every little positive thing the man does looks good in the woman's eyes. In these situations all the man has to do is not look bad. For example Larry is homely and short. He meets Joy and she isn't wowed but he is in a position where she can get to know him. He sees her every day and gives small compliments here and there. Just a little so it doesn't seem like Larry is coming on strong but enough that Joy notices. The average woman goes through the day, indeed weeks, without getting a sincere compliment. Joy gets to the point where she will start smiling when she sees Larry without him even have to say anything. Now say Larry isn't consistent with complimenting her. She notices that he only compliments her when she wears certain colors or fixes her hair in new styles. Not only will she start dressing to get those compliments but she will also get mildly aroused when he gives those compliments. After a few months Larry, a short, homely man, will arouse her more than a musclebound pretty boy. He even starts to look better to her. He grows on her. Larry is delivering the drug Joy is looking for which is that Feel Good.

See the key is for the homely or short man to accept that he is not going to deliver that instant spark. A man has to think about that long game. A man has to build that fire slowly and nurture it. He has to let that soup slow cook for a few hours, checking it every half hour to add some seasoning. An old school player once said, "A man has to put that foundation down before he can ask for the pussy." A man has to learn how to deliver that Feel Good in small doses with some subtle skill.

There you have it. Any man that's lacking in an area that he has no control over can make up for it in other areas. Any man regardless of his physical or mental blessings or shortcomings should always be in a mindset of constant self-improvement.   If man is given lemons he has to make lemonade.

Love is the Answer

September 27, 2015

I've have participated in and attended several relationship forums, workshops, and seminars over the years. I have made numerous appearances on both broadcast and Internet radio. I did several cable TV shows back in the day. I've also read more articles, forums, and blogs than I care to remember. In all that time the word "love" has been mentioned twice. One time was at a seminar conducted by one of my mentors. Another time was for an Internet radio show I used to host. I devoted a whole hour to telling my listeners that "love is the answer." In the context of solving relationship problems the word "love" has been missing.

Usually in private conversations, women will use the word "love" a lot. Only issue though is that when one listens to the context in which they are using the word they are not talking about an emotional connection where they feel bonded to a person. These women, and occasionally men, really mean they lust someone. Ninety-nine percent of the time when a woman says she no longer "loves" a man she really means she no longer lusts him. He doesn't make her vagina tingle anymore and she's off to find the next Mr. Goodbar. Let me back up a bit before I go further. Let me share a story.

My best friend and I were 15 at the time. Young teenagers who got into lots of trouble together. Nothing to go to jail over but we pushed the limits on many things. Anyway we were riding in a car with an older Black man. I mention his race because back then older Black men would give Black boys life advice whether they wanted it or not. When an elder spoke, a boy listened. We need to get back to that but I digress. The elder asked us, "What is love?" Me and my boy gave the standard romantic answers. We said it was an emotional feeling between two people, a biological urge, and several other things which were off the mark. He listened to us without interrupting and never told us we were wrong. He just told us what he considered love. He said, "Love is compassion. It is responsibility. It is forgiveness.

It is tolerance. It is admiration. It is acknowledgement." He said several other things that had nothing to do with romance. I've always kept what he said in my mind. In Black urban parlance, he gave us "good game."

As a result of talking with that elder I never confused love with lust. I could have sex with a woman and not love her. I would still treat her nice but unless I admired her I wouldn't say I loved her. On the other hand a few of the women I've loved the most I've never had sex with. Now some dumbass will probably say I was in the friendzone or something equally stupid. If a person truly loves someone it isn't dependent on what that person is doing for you sexually. You love that person for who they are. True love is to give without seeking anything in return. One of those women was the first woman to tell me she loved me. We were always platonic. It wasn't about that lust.

You know what, I can probably do a whole book getting philosophical about the meaning of the word "love" but let's just use it in the context of male/female relationships. That context is about the connection. If one doesn't agree with anything else we should be able to agree that love is about a connection, a bond between two people. That bond is not really promoted in relationship discussions. That bond is emotional in nature. It's not based on lust though it can play a part. It's not based on logic though it can play a part. So why do I mention lust and logic? The reason is that most relationship discussions and offered solutions focus on these two aspects.

There are many people, both professional relationship experts and regular folks, who believe that a man and woman should connect based on similar values, racial background, socio-economic backgrounds, educational attainment, careers, religious views, and even credit scores. They feel like people have the best chance of making a relationship successful if their value system is similar. Strong arguments for this. The relationship will be more practical. Almost like businesses merging. Two major problems though. One is that relationships based on logic tend to lack passion. Two people who have a lot in common are not necessarily attracted to each other physically. Physical attraction is a major piece in a sexual relationship. The second problem is that any change in values spell the end of the relationship. For example a male attorney and a female accountant get married. Let's say the sex life is normal so there is at least some passion. The main reason that the female married the male was that he was an attorney and they came from similar backgrounds. All of a sudden the male decides he doesn't want to be an attorney anymore. He wants to downsize and be an urban farmer. The female didn't sign up for that. They soon divorce.

Without true love, a real connection, any changes in a relationship based on logic will likely spell the end of that relationship.

There are a growing number of experts who focus on the sexual side of relationships. While I believe this to be important as I myself focus a lot on sexual development there are still problems with a relationship based solely on passion. The sex is great but regardless of how beautiful or sexy a partner is boredom will set in. I always give a relationship based on pure lust a good six months. And that's stretching it. No matter how hot the sex is the fire will die down after the two people get used to each other and life starts to intrude on the festivities. When people get together long enough any incompatibility or clash in values will lead to the end of a relationship. Even in situations where in addition to the passion there is emotional and value compatibility there are issues that can lead to a breakup. Say a man and woman meet, have passionate sex for a long time and then get married. The sex stays hot for the first few years because both people maintain sensual body builds. The problem is that it's extremely hard to maintain those body builds. Very few men can maintain a muscular body past the age of thirty. That gut starts to expand after working forty hour weeks and watching the game on Sundays. Women pop out that first baby and all of a sudden she starts to expand. The sex life that started off hot and heavy fizzles down to virtually nothing. They are simply not physically attracted to each other anymore. In some cases such a couple will get a divorce.

Without true love, a real connection, any changes in a relationship based on lust will likely spell the end of that relationship.

What true love does is two primary things. The first thing is that it balances out logic and love in a relationship.

Think about it. Love is represented by the human heart. The heart is at the halfway point between the head, which represents logic, and the sex organs, which represent lust. With true love a person can be with someone who could maybe stand to lose a few pounds and yet that person will still be seen as sexually attractive. Looking at someone through loving eyes makes them more attractive to the beholder. Even a person's "flaws" are beautiful to someone who loves them.

With true love a person can be with someone who may be of a different social class, racial group, or educational attainment level. The differences are not something that can break the couple apart. They are seen as something to learn and grow from. Remember what the elder told me, "Love is tolerance." The differences are seen as attractive through loving eyes.

The second primary thing true love does is keep people together even when changes occur in a relationship. The only inevitable thing in life is change. Nothing stays the same. Not even a person's body. With the death and birth of cells, every person has a new body every seven years. Nothing is static. Relationships will change. Things will happen. True love keeps people together through the changes. Indeed changes are welcome by mentally healthy people because it means they are growing. Sometimes a plain looking person with a loving mate can grow into a drop dead gorgeous person. Sometimes a person with a few negative personality traits can turn those negatives into positives with the right type of love.

Love is powerful but we don't want to talk about it because many people think it's corny. Many of us would rather rely on sterile studies and dubious statistics to make relationship decisions. They want practical relationships. When they manage to get a practical relationship they are still dissatisfied. Yet many say we need to be more logical. Except it's not working. For all the relationship experts, studies, questionnaires, and online dating, more people are alienated than ever.

Some experts think we need to just improve sexual skills. Despite their efforts the number of people who are involuntarily celibate is quite high. Even the people having sex are not satisfied. There are numerous books, videos, and workshops on sexual techniques yet many people don't even get to practice them. Even when they have sex in many cases there is no connection. Love even makes sex better and I don't mean lust masquerading as love. The sex is simply better when there is a connection between two people beyond what they're doing in the bedroom.

I was talking with an old friend of mine recently. Now this dude is one of the few men from whom I learned anything useful about women. This man is one the few men I have met in life who was truly good at seduction. Most players are only successful with women because of initial physical attraction. My old friend is a cat that can be in the friendzone with a woman for months and still end up sleeping with her.   During our conversation he said something that stuck with me. He said, "At the end of the day I want to come home to somebody who gives a fuck about me." This man is in his fifties and has women young and old who will travel from out of state to see him. Thing is he had the right perspective. It's not about being a player with a high notch count. At the end of the day it's about being with a person who gives a fuck what happens to you. See that's real love. We all need it and it's not corny to say so. It's real talk.

About the Author

Rom Wills is the author of several books including the international bestseller, Nice Guys and Players. Rom is an author, a blogger, a podcaster, and all around Renaissance man. His most important job is being a father to two teenaged boys.

Follow Rom on the World Wide Web:

www.romwills.com
Facebook.com/Willspublishing
Twitter: @RomWills1
Instagram: @romwills
www.connectpal.com/romwillsraw
www.patreon.com/romwills
nice-guys-and-players-university.teachable.com
www.youtube.com/user/Romwills

CPSIA information can be obtained
at www.ICGtesting.com
Printed in the USA
LVHW080909071120
671027LV00063B/2155